TRIBUTE TO FERRARI

TRIBUTE TO FERRARI
AN EXHIBITION AHEAD OF ITS TIME

Fondation *Cartier*
pour l'art contemporain

This publication recounts the exhibition created
in tribute to Enzo Ferrari by the Fondation
Cartier pour l'art contemporain, and presented
from May 22 to August 30, 1987 at the Domaine
du Montcel in Jouy-en-Josas.

TRIBUTE TO FERRARI
An exhibition initiated by
Alain Dominique Perrin,
President of the Fondation Cartier
pour l'art contemporain,
and Marie-Claude Beaud,
Director from 1984 to 1994,
designed by Andrée Putman
—

Edited by
Philippe Séclier

In spring 1986, a year or so after having founded and inaugurated the Fondation Cartier pour l'art contemporain at the Domaine du Montcel in Jouy-en-Josas, I wanted to put together a large-scale exhibition paying homage to Ferrari. A year later, nearly fifty of the remarkable, legendary cars arrived to spend the summer on the grounds of the Fondation Cartier. The exhibition, a watershed in its approach to exhibiting contemporary design, was widely celebrated and became a huge popular success with nearly ninety thousand visitors over three months.

I had first met Enzo Ferrari in 1982, and we had often seen each other over the years. Little by little, during our discussions, it became clear to me that we should bring together our two houses, Cartier and Ferrari, which were—and remain—two of the most prestigious in the world. "You are an icon of your time," I told him during one of our conversations. "Your cars and engines are works of art and you are one of the greatest artists of the twentieth century." To which he replied: "Sono solo un meccanico (I am just a mechanic)."

After Enzo Ferrari agreed to the idea of the exhibition, I appointed the then head of the Fondation Cartier, Marie-Claude Beaud, as its director. She travelled from Modena to Maranello, Turin to Mas du Clos, to oversee and organize the exhibition *Tribute to Ferrari* with immense curiosity and extraordinary enthusiasm. She and Andrée Putman, who designed the exhibition's scenography, imagined *Tribute to Ferrari* like a dream in which the Ferraris had been parachuted into the middle of the park, a dream through which to rediscover the history of a saga and the worlds of racing and design.

In 1987, Enzo Ferrari honored us by becoming the patron of this first exhibition dedicated to the Prancing Horse. Thirty-eight years later, this book tells its story and relates its profound impact on the history of the Fondation Cartier and that of contemporary design. PARIS, 2025

ALAIN DOMINIQUE PERRIN
PRESIDENT OF THE FONDATION CARTIER POUR L'ART CONTEMPORAIN

Some might consider it anachronistic to exhibit automobiles, even Ferraris, in a contemporary art foundation. And yet, from the outset, this project enthused the Fondation's entire team. Everyone was searching for a previously unseen model or an extremely rare photograph—in short, it was an effervescence that perhaps strangely resembles the feeling that reigns in the Ferrari pit during a Grand Prix. The object itself is seductive: its forms, of course, but also the color, repeated to the point of obsession, and the noise. That famous Ferrari noise, which all Ferrari lovers, particularly Jack Setton, told me would be spectacular and exceptional.

I was skeptical... until I took my first "drive" in a Ferrari, at Mas du Clos in the Creuse; on the track, in the company of the owner of this fabulous collection. My palms were a little sweaty when I got out of the car, but I had managed to make small talk at each turn, to give the impression that all was well. However, everyone was right: the noise—the soft, muffled sound that becomes piercing and remarkable—definitely contributes to the legend.

Then it was on to Maranello. Well, I told myself, we're going to the holy of holies, the Mecca of the car. I had already met great artists like Picasso, De Kooning, or Beuys, and now it was the Commendatore. We'll see, I said to myself! What struck me most was his washed-out gaze, suddenly peeking out from behind his sunglasses, sizing up and weighing up those around him, then jaunty and affectionate when he looked at Maria Grazia Colico, the indispensable go-between for the Fondation and Ferrari while we put this tribute together. I realized that it was all a question of loyalty and complicity, his anger as much as his joy, his acceptance and his rejection.

Sometime later, chatting with Daniel Marin, Antoine Prunet, and Claude Vialard, I sensed how, for these three Ferrari lovers, the formidable will to win the next day was linked to Enzo Ferrari's exceptional relationship to history and time. In that moment, the parallels with the world of art were clear, and consequently we were in the same space: that of creation. More than the culmination of a form that the harmony between Pininfarina and Ferrari has perfected, more than the human ingenuity and the engine performance fine-tuned by the engineers, more than the genius of certain drivers who have brought so many victories, it is the "conductor" who matters: that extraordinary poet, Enzo Ferrari.

The intention of this exhibition is now obvious: to steer the visitor through the history of a legend on to the world of racing and design and the ultimate dream of "possess a Ferrari"—if only with the eyes! Andrée Putman was able to transcribe this journey to perfection. As lacking in confidence in four-wheeled machines as I was, she too was charmed by this magical name. Photographers also succumbed, going from novices to Ferrari lovers. The anachronism mentioned at the beginning of this text is no longer an issue. With this exhibition, we are presenting the story of one of the greatest names in the world of automobiles, but above all and without contest, we are showcasing the work of a genius of contemporary creation. JOUY-EN-JOSAS, MAY 1987

MARIE-CLAUDE BEAUD
DIRECTOR OF THE FONDATION CARTIER POUR L'ART CONTEMPORAIN FROM 1984 TO 1994

Fig 1 Enzo Ferrari in his office in Maranello, Italy, April 1987.
Portrait by Pierre-Olivier Deschamps for the Fondation Cartier pour l'art contemporain.

ENZO FERRARI
LIVING FOR THE RACE

Jean-Louis Moncet

Journalist

Enzo Ferrari once said at one of his annual press conferences, which were renowned in the car world: "Sono un ragazzo della periferia modenese, è la verità" (I'm just a boy from the outskirts of Modena, that's the truth).

How did a boy named Enzo build an industrial empire over the course of the twentieth century and make the name Ferrari synonymous with art and luxury? How did this man know how to bring together the trades of mechanic and craftsman, combining the thrill of sport with the beauty of forms, so often opposites, like hot and cold?

Cold, precisely. "The cold, real cold has been like the common denominator of my life in its most important moments," Ferrari wrote. "I was born in Modena, officially on February 20, 1898, although really it was on the 18th; the snow lay so deep that month, so my mother has told me, that it was only possible to get to the Registry Office two days after I was born."[1] This is how Ferrari described his cold arrival in the world; the hot did not take long to become part of his character. The first car race he attended, aged ten, with his father and elder brother Alfredo, was in Bologna in 1908. He remembers that the circuit, which crossed the city on Via Persicetana and Via Emilia, made "a great impression" on him. Then, aged seventeen, he saw the photograph of a driver who had won the Indianapolis 500 in an Italian newspaper. His name: Raffaele "Ralph" DePalma, driving a Mercedes. Again, Ferrari was enthralled.

The First World War took a heavy toll on the Ferrari family as the young Enzo lost his father, then his brother, Alfredo. After his military service and despite a recommendation from the army, he could not find a job with Fiat, the leading Italian constructor, and he found himself alone and cold in the Turin snow. He finally found a job with a mechanic, before joining Costruzione Meccaniche Nazionali (CMN), thanks to Ugo Sivocci, a racing driver with whom he was friendly. His salary was low, but his enthusiasm and sense of vocation were high.

1. Enzo Ferrari. *Piloti, che gente...* (Bologna: Conti Editore, 1987).

Fig 2

Fig 3

His first result as a race driver was soon in: fourth in a hill-climb race between Parma and Poggio di Berceto on October 5, 1919. In 1920, he moved to Alfa Romeo, the manufacturer that used competitive racing as an aid to the construction of its cars.

Enzo Ferrari enjoyed a string of victories, including one in 1923 at a race in Ravenna, where he met the Count Baracca. Later the Countess Paolina Baracca suggested that he emblazons his cars with the equine emblem of their late fighter-pilot son, Francesco. "The horse was, and has remained, black," he wrote "but I added the gold field, this being the color of Modena."[2]

Six years later, at the end of 1929, he suggested to three racing driver friends that they set up a team that would pool transport, mechanics, and their resources. The team was to be called Mutina, reminiscent of the name of Modena in latin, but the team's notary asked, "Why not Ferrari?" On November 16, 1929, during the new company's first board meeting, a fund of 200,000 lire was created to allow participation in Italian road race Mille Miglia.[3] The brand-new Scuderia Ferrari got to work.

The team gradually took over full responsibility for Alfa Romeo's racing activities, which would later become Alfa Corse. The Scuderia raced with the best Italian drivers, as well as excellent Frenchmen, including René Dreyfus, Guy Moll, and the Monégasque Louis Chiron. On July 9 and 10, 1932, at the 24 Hours of Spa-Francorchamps in Belgium, the first Alfa Romeos bearing the *cavallino rampante*—the famous little prancing horse—made their appearance.

In January that year, Enzo Ferrari had hung up his racing suit after the birth of his son, Dino. "At the time, I already had my doubts," he remembered. "Reasonable doubts because I had a major handicap: I was driving the car with respect. And if you want to get great results, you have to know how to mistreat it."[4] Enzo Ferrari became full-time team boss. While the Scuderia Ferrari was nominally based in Modena, the majority of its work was in Milan, at Alfa Romeo. Ferrari remained there until 1939,

Fig 2 Francesco Baracca in front of his fighter jet bearing the *cavallino rampante* (Prancing Horse) emblem.

Fig 3 The building of the new Scuderia Ferrari, Viale Trento Trieste, Modena, 1929.

2. Enzo Ferrari, *The Enzo Ferrari Story* (MacMillan, 1964), p. 27.
3. The Mille Miglia was one of the world's most famous endurance races. Organized twenty-four times between 1927 and 1957, the 24-hour event was run on open roads between Brescia and Rome.
4. Ferrari, *Piloti*.

Fig 4

Fig 4 Enzo Ferrari and mechanic Michele Conti in an Alfa Romeo 20-40 HP, 1920.

5. The 1940 edition of the Mille Miglia, held on April 28, was nine circuits of circular route running Brescia-Mantova-Cremona-Brescia.

working with engineer Gioacchino Colombo to build the Alfa Romeo 158. That car—and its 159 variant—would see great success after the war in the first season of the World Drivers' Championship (now Formula 1) in 1950–51 with Alfa Romeo's first two world titles.

In early 1939, Enzo Ferrari quit Alfa Romeo following a falling-out and returned to Modena. The non-competition contract he had signed with the Milanese company prevented him from building a car under his own name, so he simply founded a new company called Auto-Avio Costruzioni and set about creating what would become the Type 815, with its straight V8 engine in an elegant Touring Superleggera body. This "*anteprima* Ferrari,*"* as it is known today, took part in the 1940 Mille Miglia, a truncated version of the race, with drivers Lotario Rangoni and Alberto Ascari.[5] When World War II broke out, machine tools across Italy were set to work at full capacity. In 1943, Enzo Ferrari moved his large workshops 15 kilometers from Modena to a small, now world-famous town: Maranello. (The Scuderia's address remained Viale Trento e Trieste in Modena, however.)

Fig 5

Fig 6

Prancing horse, Maranello: these words conjure up all the imagery associated with Enzo Ferrari, a man always driven by his immense passion for motor racing, an all-consuming passion that animated him throughout his life, though never to the detriment of his reputation or behavior, lifestyle, or wealth, even if he did live modestly.

When peace returned, sporting events quickly restarted and race lovers brought out the cars they had hidden since 1939. In 1948, the Commission Sportive Internationale (CSI) of the Fédération Internationale de l'Automobile (FIA) issued a ruling that created rules for race cars. Rather than name these categories, disciplines or series, the CSI chose to call them formulas: the most powerful cars raced in Formula 1; the less powerful in Formula 2; with Formula 3 for beginners. It was these rules that were used for the first Formula 1 World Drivers' Championship, organized in 1950 and 1951.

Enzo Ferrari immediately joined the FIA, which was now the supreme authority for motoring, and he never left. The Alfa Romeo 158 and 159—the "Alfette"—dominated in 1950 and 1951 making Giuseppe "Nino" Farina and Juan Manuel Fangio the first two world champions in history. Enzo Ferrari could congratulate himself for these world titles and cars for the good reason that he and engineer Gioacchino Colombo had designed these machines.

For the first two seasons, the CSI chose a simple technical formula: Formula 1 cars had to be equipped with either a 1.5-liter supercharged or a 4.5-liter naturally aspirated engine. Enzo Ferrari remembered admiring the V12 engines that American manufacturer Packard put in its sedans that were luxurious and fast (170 kmph/105 mph). The engine so impressed him that he began working with Aurelio Lampredi, his new engine designer, to develop his own version.

In September 1946, Ferrari undertook his first tests with his new engine and while Enzo Ferrari did build V4, V6, and V8 engines, the V12 became a Maranello trademark. On May 25, 1947, a Ferrari 125 S with a V12 achieved its first victory, driven by Franco Cortese, on the Terme di

Fig 5 Showcase of Alfa Romeo cars from the Scuderia Ferrari, 1932.

Fig 6 Enzo Ferrari at the wheel of a 125 S during the car's first tests, March 12, 1947.

Fig 7

Fig 8

Fig 7 Enzo Ferrari (second right) and his son Alfredo (first left), aka Dino, observing an engine assembly, 1947.

Fig 8 Juan Manuel Fangio and Enzo Ferrari during practice for the Italian Grand Prix in Monza, September 4, 1960. That year, Fangio became world champion for the fourth time, and for the first time in a Ferrari, the D50.

Caracalla street circuit in Rome. On October 12 that year, French driver Raymond Sommer won the Turin Grand Prix. "I remember the shock of that victory,"[6] wrote Enzo Ferrari. The reign of the V12 had begun.

The best was yet to come, though. The World Drivers' Championship began in 1950. On July 14, 1951, the British Grand Prix was held at Silverstone. Alfa Romeo had dominated the early season with its in-line supercharged V8, but at Silverstone, Argentine driver Froilán González won driving a 4.5-liter Ferrari 375, 50 seconds ahead of the Alfa Romeo 158 driven by his friend and compatriot Fangio. In his autobiography, Enzo Ferrari, no doubt remembering that he was the man behind the Alfa engine before the war, wrote: "I wept with joy, but my tears of happiness were blended with tears of sadness, for I thought that day, 'I have killed my mother!'"[7]

For 1952 and 1953, the FIA decided that the constructors' championship would no longer be run for Formula 1, but rather Formula 2. Ferrari was ready for the change with the fabulous 500 F2 and its 2-liter in-line V4 engine, which would go on to dominate the Formula 2 championship with a future star behind the wheel: Alberto Ascari.

Enzo Ferrari was at the top of his game, his fame spreading. Yet he was also suffering in silence. His son, Alfredo, nicknamed Alfredino and Dino, was already showing signs of muscular dystrophy, a degenerative condition. A trained engineer, Dino worked closely with the best motor engineers at Maranello before his death in 1956. His memory still lives on in all the engines, Grand Prix race cars, and GT cars that have been named after him. Today, Enzo Ferrari's legacy is carried by Piero, Enzo's second son, born in 1945, who worked with his father in the Maranello workshops.

Before he entered and won in Formula 1, Enzo Ferrari had understood which discipline every manufacturer, even the smallest, had to concentrate their efforts on: endurance races. In these events, manufacturers had to prove their cars' quality and ability to run smoothly, reliably, flexibly, and fast. The races were generating renown and worldwide

6. Ferrari, *Piloti.*
7. Ferrari, *The Enzo Ferrari Story*, p. 20.

Fig 9

Fig 10

excitement, from the Daytona 24 Hours to the 12 Hours of Sebring in Florida, the Carrera Panamericana in Mexico, and above all, the 24 Hours of Le Mans. Until 1973, Ferrari entered cars into all the major endurance races, putting celebrated drivers in ultra-fast cars that were designed for speed and were, of course, extremely striking.

One of these races was particularly close to Ferrari's heart, however: the Mille Miglia. "No driver could call himself complete if his laurels did not include a victory at Brescia," he wrote in his autobiography.[8] An industrial city in Lombardy, less than 100 kilometers from Milan, Brescia was the Mille Miglia's start and finish, and there was a Ferrari on the starting grid from 1948, the team's first entry seeing its first victory with Clemente Biondetti behind the wheel. Until the race's final edition in 1957, Ferrari won the prestigious Mille Miglia eight times. It is no surprise that certain models of Ferrari were badged "MM."

While a Formula 1 car is only attractive if it wins, a sports car prototype and its beautiful forms always moves lovers of art and speed. Which is why these cars are so appealing to collectors, an aesthetic attraction that has become even stronger today. An endurance car also has a significant advantage over Formula 1 cars: it has an autonomous starter—that's the rule—so does not need a battery of electrical devices to get its engine going.

Racing was becoming increasingly expensive, a fact that Enzo Ferrari had long understood. As far back as 1950, when the first Grand Prix in the history of the World Championship was set to be held at Silverstone, Ferrari decided to send his cars to a little-known speed race in Mons, Belgium, where the organizers were paying better starting bonuses.

Fig 9 Phil Hill and Enzo Ferrari during tests at the Italian Grand Prix in Monza, September 6, 1958.

Fig 10 Entrance to the Ferrari factory, Maranello, 1957.

8. Ferrari, *The Enzo Ferrari Story*, p. 165.

"It is in the awareness of this torment for technical innovation and in the creations derived from it that I found, amid infinite toils, my own lifelong religion."[9]

ENZO FERRARI

Legend has it that the gatekeeper at the Maranello factory was instructed to lift the barrier only if a paid bill was presented as an exit pass. In 1973, one of Enzo Ferrari's advisors, Peter Schetty, a Swiss businessman and Scuderia hill-climb and endurance driver, presented the Commendatore with a dilemma. With Ferrari losing the 1973 endurance world championship to Matra, and without a world Formula 1 title winner since 1964, Schetty had concluded that the Scuderia no longer had the means to compete in two championships. A choice had to be made. The future, according to Peter Schetty, belonged to Formula 1, a format more adapted to television and with a growing worldwide reputation into the bargain. Enzo Ferrari had no choice but to opt for Grand Prix racing—a necessity for the future.

How were the road-going Ferrari, the celebrated GT, the refined Gran Turismo, born? Since the early days, Ferrari had thought about money, which had been cruelly lacking during his childhood. To finance the racing, he had long been obliged to sell certain cars, particularly race cars, to young wealthy men who dreamed of racing fame. In 1963, its precarious financial situation saw Henry Ford II try to buy Ferrari, that synonym of victory and excellence. Luckily, the head of Fiat, Gianni Agnelli, a visionary about the future of Maranello, came to the rescue, and Fiat took over Ferrari instead.

Another aspect of Enzo Ferrari's attempts to secure his company's future was the decision to write another chapter by adapting his race cars for road use. Many master bodywork companies were already working on Ferrari models, including Carrozzeria Boana, Zagato, Carrozzeria Allemano, Carrozzeria Vignale, and Bertone. The two giants

9. *La Gazzetta dello Sport,* January 11, 1975.

Fig 11   Fig 12

were undoubtedly Scaglietti and Pininfarina, founded by Gian-Battista Pinin Farina. "Ferrari understood that his cars needed a specific image," recalled Battista's son, Sergio Pininfarina. "He thought my father could help him realize his idea, even if it meant discussions with a character who was not always easy..."

From the drawing boards emerged the *manichini* and hammered aluminum, tarmac-devouring machines with intoxicating shapes. Journalist and test driver José Rosinski always used to call road Ferraris the ultimate expression of "nobility of color and V12, double-OHC mechanics." This status made them not only collectors' items, but also pieces of world heritage, a legacy Enzo Ferrari's successor, Luca di Montezemolo, was able to preserve.

To continue producing his "beloved race cars," he was once again never short of ideas, using his image as the austere master of Maranello to put on performances. Instead of trying to sell his GTs to customers, he made them come to him and made them wait. In the process, he transformed his facilities at Maranello into the backstage of what is today known as the jet set. Crowned heads of state, political and religious leaders, movie actors and actresses, TV stars, billionaire industrialists, and writers all passed through his *ingeniere*'s office, where he would receive them and tell them with a certain art and polite condescension exactly what they wanted to hear. He summed up in one line how he felt about all the precious time lost to this procession of celebrities: "Maranello, a disaster."

Nevertheless, he would always call journalists himself ("I attach considerable importance to their visits"[10]). He adored this way of communicating, fond as he was of press coverage, but rarely seen on television.

Fig 11 Phil Hill during a test session for the 256 F1 in Modena, 1960, in the presence of engineer Carlo Chiti and Enzo Ferrari (right).

Fig 12 Enzo Ferrari (center) and designer Gian-Battista Pinin Farina (left) in the Ferrari factories of Maranello, 1960.

10. Ferrari, *The Enzo Ferrari Story*, p. 138.

The ceremony was unchanging. He would sit down, his advisors standing behind him, hand out a few figures and discuss victories and defeats. Woe betide anyone who complained about not seeing an Italian driving a Ferrari. In a thunderous and angry voice, the *ingeniere* would remind the impudent journalist just how much he had been pilloried by the Italian press over the years for the dramatic and fatal accidents involving his cars.

Once calm had returned, he would pull a small folder towards him and open it to reveal carefully cut clippings. He would name the newspaper and the journalist who had written whatever he found erroneous, and the offending journalist would bow his or her head, fully reprimanded. When the meeting was over, everyone would rise and pass one by one in front of Signor Ferrari's desk and shake his hand, not forgetting to ask after their family or their son's studies. The court before its king.

During these press conferences, the regulars would look forward to the wrong question from the novice taking his first steps into the inner sanctum: "Signor Ferrari, which of your victories was your favorite?" or "Mr. Ferrari, what do you consider to be the best Ferrari ever built?" To these questions *il vecchio*, as he was respectfully nicknamed, would invariably reply: "*La prossima*"—the next. He was never one to pay attention to past glories. If the journalist wanted to chat about all the iconic cars already produced at Maranello, he would most often refer the person to the great collectors, often citing Pierre Bardinon in France.

Watching archival films of Enzo Ferrari, it's striking to observe the extent to which he marked his time. Yet, he did not invent the color red for his cars; it was the Italian national color. He didn't design his cars' bodies; they were the pencil strokes of Italian master coachbuilders. The V12 engine, his obsession, was not his design, but his engineers'. Even the *cavallino*—the little prancing horse—was not his. Indeed, it is not unreasonable to conclude that above all Enzo Ferrari's real talent was as an agitator of ideas.

Sono lieto che la Ferrari sia presente alla

Fondation Cartier pour l'Art Contemporain e

qui interpreti il rapporto macchina-uomo non

soltanto come fatto industriale, ma anche

come espressione artistica.   *Ferrari*

Fig 1

Fig 1 Letter from Enzo Ferrari addressed to the Fondation Cartier pour l'art contemporain, 1987:
"I am delighted that Ferrari is being presented at the Fondation Cartier pour l'art contemporain and
that the relationship between man and car is being shown not just from an industrial point of view, but
also as an artistic expression."

AN EXHIBITION AHEAD OF ITS TIME

Philippe Séclier

Former journalist, editor

This is the story of an exhibition that rolled out the red carpet for Ferrari and its most striking road and race cars, and celebrated the company's founder, Enzo Ferrari, the man with the tinted glasses and the "Bourbon nose." It is also the story of an exhibition about design and speed that verged on the outrageous thanks to an aerial design created for a park fifteen miles southwest of Paris. Finally, it is the story of an exhibition that caused a sensation in the contemporary art world. That exhibition was *Tribute to Ferrari*, held in 1987, but whose history had begun five years earlier. In 1982, Alain Dominique Perrin, recently appointed CEO at Cartier and Cartier International, was invited by Enzo Ferrari to make a first visit to Maranello, the kingdom of the Prancing Horse. The Commendatore wanted to distribute his own range of Ferrari accessories to put an end to rampant counterfeiting, so he turned to this young businessman who had already launched the successful Must de Cartier line. The two bosses began meeting regularly. "Between 1982 and 1985, I met him at least five times a year," remembers Alain Dominique Perrin. "Enzo loved the Must line."[1] On April 15, 1983, a press conference was organized at the Italian manufacturer's headquarters during which Enzo Ferrari and Alain Dominique Perrin publicly announced their partnership. An exclusive license was granted to Cartier to produce and market Ferrari Formula, a range of high-quality accessories, including watches, chronographs, glasses, pens, key rings, and small leather goods.

A year later, in 1984, Alain Dominique Perrin founded the Fondation Cartier pour l'art contemporain. His friend, the sculptor César,[2] had convinced him of the need for a "free and different" exhibition space,

1. Alain Dominique Perrin (born in 1942) was chair of the Cartier company from 1975 to 1998. From 1999 to 2003, he was vice-chair of the Swiss luxury group Richemont. A major collector and art lover, he created the Fondation Cartier in 1984 and is still its chair today.
2. César Baldaccini, aka César (1921–1998), was a French sculptor and member of the New Realism movement, famous for its use of recycled materials and notably compressions of automobiles.

Fig 2

Fig 3

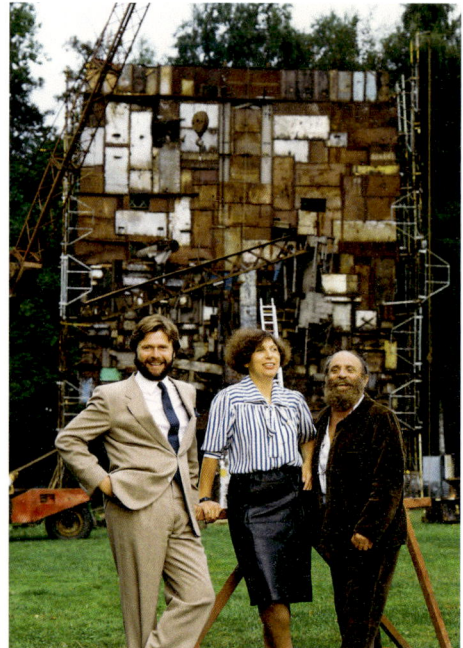

Fig 4

and suggested meeting Jean Hamon, patron of the arts and real-estate developer, who then owned the Domaine du Montcel, in Jouy-en-Josas. Situated in the Bièvre Valley, two and half miles south of Versailles, this wooded park was dominated by a château that had once belonged to the Oberkampf family, whose factory manufacturing Jouy fabric, founded in 1759, had made the name of this village of seven thousand inhabitants. Another source of pride was the Montcel School, a private school and center of excellence that had educated, notably, painter Gérard Garouste, singer Michel Sardou, director Jean-Michel Ribes, and writer and Nobel Prize winner Patrick Modiano.[3]

A great lover of contemporary art, Jean Hamon had ordered a sculpture from Arman that had been installed in the park in 1982: *Long Term Parking* was a rectangular concrete tower in which were embedded no fewer than fifty-nine cars, including popular models such as a Fiat 126; Peugeot 204 and 404; Mercedes 200 D; Citroën GS; Chrysler 160; Fiat 500; Renault 4, 5, 6, and 12; Panhard Ami 6; Volkswagen Beetle; BMW 2002; and Simca 1000. In 1983, César had been commissioned to produce *Hommage à Eiffel*, a gigantic eighteen-meter-high slab created from fragments of a steel staircase recovered from a Parisian tower block. Almost as high as the tops of the surrounding trees, the work was finally completed and installed in 1989. Alain Dominique Perrin decided to rent the fourteen-hectare site at Domaine du Montcel to show solo and thematic exhibitions, and to welcome young French and international artists in residence; these would go on to include Fabrice Hyber, Jean-Michel Othoniel, Chéri Samba, Cai Guo-Qiang, and Huang Yong Ping. On César's advice, he appointed Marie-Claude Beaud, then curator at Musée d'Art

Fig 2 Enzo Ferrari (in the foreground) and Alain Dominique Perrin during a ceremony held for Enzo Ferrari's eighty-fifth birthday, in Modena, Italy, 1983.

Fig 3 Domaine du Montcel in Jouy-en-Josas, 1984.

Fig 4 Alain Dominique Perrin, Marie-Claude Beaud, and César in front of the *Hommage à Eiffel* under construction, Jouy-en-Josas, 1984.

3. From 1923 to 1980, the site hosted the École du Montcel, to which Patrick Modiano made reference in two of his novels: *Such Fine Boys*, trans. Mark Polizzotti (Yale University Press, 2017) and *Pedigree: A Memoir*, trans. Mark Polizzotti (Yale University Press, 2015).

Fig 5

Fig 5 A Testarossa (1984) and a 312 T4 (1979) during the installation of the *Tribute to Ferrari* exhibition. In the background, the sculpture *Long-Term Parking* (1982) by Arman, which is permanently installed in the park.

AN EXHIBITION AHEAD OF ITS TIME

HOMMAGE A FERRARI

DU 22 MAI AU 26 JUILLET 1987

FONDATION *Cartier* POUR L'ART CONTEMPORAIN

Fig 6

Fig 6 Cover of the special issue of the magazine *Automobiles Classiques*, no. 19, 1987.
Photograph by Emmanuel Zurini, 1,000 km of Monza, 1969.

Fig 7

Fig 7 Invitation to the opening of the *Tribute to Ferrari* exhibition.

4. Marie-Claude Beaud (1946–2024) directed the Fondation Cartier pour l'art contemporain (1984–1994), the American Center (1994–1996), the musées de l'Union centrale des arts décoratifs (1996–1999), the Mudam Luxembourg (2000–2008), and the Nouveau Musée national de Monaco (2009–2021).
5. Philip Johnson (1906–2005) was the first director of the department of architecture and design at the MoMA, from 1932 to 1936, then again from 1946 to 1954.

in Toulon, as artistic director.[4] On October 20, 1984, the first exhibition at the Fondation Cartier pour l'art contemporain, *Les Fers de César*, was opened by then minister of culture Jack Lang. Eighteen months later, in summer 1986, *Les Années 60: 1960-1969, la décade triomphante* was a resounding success. "I asked Marie-Claude to curate interdisciplinary exhibitions for the general public each summer," says Alain Dominique Perrin. "I didn't ever want the Fondation Cartier to be categorized as a museum. That word was banned in our conversations. We had to set ourselves apart from the cultural scene." Which is how, in fall 1986, the idea of an exhibition dedicated to Ferrari was born. "I loved the brand, and I had even owned a few of their cars," remembers Alain Dominique Perrin, "but it was Enzo's character, what he had done with his company and with his own hands, particularly in the early days, and then what it had become over time, that really made me want to make this proposal. During one of our last meetings, he asked me why I wanted to exhibit Ferrari. I told him: 'Because you are an icon of your time. Your cars and engines are works of art and you are one of the greatest artists of the twentieth century.' To which he replied, 'Sono solo un meccanico.' 'Yes, but a mechanic of genius,' I retorted. As no other exhibition had ever been devoted to him, he was enormously flattered. I spoke to Marie-Claude Beaud, who loved the idea and took it all in hand."

Tribute to Ferrari might have been the first major retrospective devoted to the manufacturer from Maranello, but there had already been shows bringing together the worlds of art and automobiles. In 1951 at MoMA in New York, for example, American architect Philip Johnson[5] had curated *Eight Automobiles,* for which Mercedes, Bentley, Cisitalia,

Fig 8

Fig 9

and Talbot were invited; Ferrari was not.[6] The exhibition *Bolide Design*, organized at the Musée des Art Décoratifs in Paris in 1970, allowed the public to discover a Ferrari 330 P3/4 belonging to French collector Pierre Bardinon, as well as prototypes including a 512 S and a P6. In 1984, the Museum of Contemporary Art in Los Angeles presented *Automobile and Culture*, and two years later, the Haus der Kunst in Munich followed suit with the exhibition *Das Automobil in der Kunst: 1886–1986*. But once again, no trace of Ferrari. The Fondation Cartier pour l'art contemporain was thinking big. Forty-five sports cars—Gran Turismo and competition models featuring the *cavallino rampante*, including Formula 1 cars—were to be brought together for the occasion. There would also be models from Italian design studio Pininfarina, prototypes, engines—notably His Highness the V12—and a whole gallery of portraits of the drivers who had written the history of Ferrari. Finally, ten photographers would be commissioned, including Frank Horvat, Jeanloup Sieff, and Franco Fontana, to respond to the question, "What does Ferrari mean to you?"

Marie-Claude Beaud called on Andrée Putman for the scenography.[7] For the show, the high priestess of French design, who saw the world in black and white, had to deal with a different color. "We didn't have carte blanche, but carte rouge!" Marie-Claude Beaud says. "With a company like that, we had to keep in mind the historical aspects, as well as, of course, the technical and the aesthetic. Above all, we had to work with people's passionate relationship with Ferrari. Andrée and I were constantly exchanging ideas. It was really thoughtful, very technical. She asked questions and raised problems that were going to come up. Everything was planned." Except the unforeseen, obviously. Andrée Putman delegated

Fig 8 and 9 Preparatory drawings made by Bruno Moinard for Andrée Putman's scenography, October 1986.

6. Thanks to a donation from Ferrari in 1993, MoMA acquired the 641 driven by Alain Prost during the Formula 1 World Championship of 1990. On this occasion, the New York museum presented the exhibition *Design for Speed: Three Automobiles by Ferrari* from November 4, 1993 to April 4, 1994, six years after the *Tribute to Ferrari* exhibition. The two other models were the 166 MM Barchetta and the F40.

7. Andrée Putman (1925–2013) was a French interior architect and designer internationally renowned for her elegant and minimalist style. *Tribute to Ferrari* is the only exhibition for which she devised the scenography for the Fondation Cartier.

Fig 10

8. The design office had twenty-two associates at that time.

the operational production of this concept to Bruno Moinard, then a young designer on her team.[8] "Andrée wasn't someone who designed per se," says Bruno Moinard. "She was a great stylist; she knew how to assemble objects sublimely. All her creativity, her inventiveness, lay in the collision of objects. She talked to me, told me stories, and I drew. She told me, 'A car is a child's dream.' So we imagined how these Ferraris had arrived at night by air in baskets. The next morning, we'd awake with these red sports cars dotted around this huge green park. Andrée descended from the Montgolfier family, so we followed the thread of that idea. Even if I also draw merry-go-rounds." Bruno Moinard quickly decided to get in touch with a certain Mr. Lemarchand, a manufacturer of hot-air balloons. "We had planned a test on the property of collector Jack Setton," he says. "Except it was snowing that day and so windy that everything was cancelled. But it gave me the opportunity to see a hot-air balloon up close. I eventually had a dozen made specially for the exhibition. My colleagues and I wondered how to keep them in the air—each balloon had to have its own ventilation system and had to be weatherproof. So we made helium balloons with an integrated windsock and a blower. We also opted for two different formats, the smaller was a cone-shaped model, and decided to place the cars on wooden railway sleepers."

Fig 11

The suspended Ferraris were to be placed around the Fondation Cartier's park, in the middle of a section called "La Route" (The Road). They were commercially available models loaned by Ferrari's French importer Charles Pozzi.[9] Daniel Marin, the company's CEO, knew Alain Dominique Perrin and as a gesture of friendship lent him these magnificent *berlinetti* and cabriolets. "At the time, Ferrari wasn't really involved in this sort of event, apart from car shows, obviously," recalls Marin. "Management had other things to worry about. But it was wonderful promotion because it was the company's very first prestige exhibition. We loaned a 212 Inter Europa Coupé, designed in 1952 by Pininfarina, a 1971 Daytona, a Dino 246 GT from 1973, a 512 BB from 1976, a 288 GTO from 1984 and a Testarossa, which had been officially unveiled at the Lido in Paris in 1984." Connected by ropes to the hot-air balloons, these Ferraris seemed lighter than ever in Bruno Moinard's drawings, almost weightless in the Domaine du Montcel, where horse-drawn carriages had once used the main gravel driveway to reach the château.

Putman and Moinard also designed the scenography of the "Bunker," situated in the northwest of the park. Made up of a central interior space open on three levels, this imposing concrete parallelepiped, built between 1943 and 1944 by the Luftwaffe, was home to the "Le Monde de

Fig 11 View of the "Bunker" harbouring the cars from Jack Setton's collection. From left to right: a 312 B2 (1971), a 312 T3 (1978), and a 312 F1 (1968).

9. Charles Pozzi (1909–2001), whose real name was Carlo Alberto Pozzi, became Ferrari's official importer in 1969. From 1971 on, the Pozzi-Ferrari France car yard brought in Ferrari 365 GTB/4, 512 BB/LM, 308 GTB Groupe 4, or F40 LM. Jean-Claude Andruet, Claude Ballot-Léna, Guy Chasseuil, and Jean-Pierre Jabouille distinguished themselves behind their wheels, in races such as the 24 Hours of Le Mans, the Tour de France Automobile, or the Tour de Corse.

Fig 12

Fig 12 Pierre Bardinon at the center of the canvas pyramid containing twenty-three cars from his collection.

10. Peter Schetty (b. 1942) was the director of Scuderia Ferrari in 1971 and 1972, the last season before he won the World Sportscar Championship.

la course" (The World of Racing) section of the exhibition. Alongside portraits of Ferrari drivers from the 1940s to the 1970s, helmets, and driving overalls, sat eight Formula 1 cars, alternatively exhibited by lack of space, that had competed in the world championship between 1955 and 1979. Their drivers had been Grand Prix legends: John Surtees, Niki Lauda, Jacky Ickx, Clay Regazzoni, and Carlos Reutemann. A 212 E Barchetta, built for hill-climbing races, which had been driven by the Swiss Peter Schetty in the 1970s, completed the list.[10] They all belonged to entrepreneur Jack Setton, who at the time also owned Formula 1 Renault and Williams cars. "He was an obsessive creator, with a profound aesthetic sense," says auctioneer Hervé Poulain, who had known Setton for many years. "Nothing could resist him, and he had to have everything perfect. His collection was exceptional." Like the collector Pierre Bardinon, Jack Setton had built his own racetrack to drive his cars on the grounds of his property, the Château de Wideville, southwest of Paris. "I always loved driving, and I always loved speed," says the businessman, first known as the French importer of Pioneer hi-fi equipment in the 1980s. "My collection was never a museum, but rather a big garage. I bought models that excited me. And really, a race car is only interesting if it has won races."

Fig 13

In the original project for the *Tribute to Ferrari* exhibition, according to a memo sent by Marie-Claude Beaud to Alain Dominique Perrin on October 27, 1986, the "Bunker" was to have been devoted to Pierre Bardinon's collection. In the end, the twenty-three rare sport and Gran Turismo Ferrari were placed under a pyramid-shaped big top. "I had suggested creating a sort of inverted circus," recalls Moinard. "At this one, it was to be the public center stage getting a close-up view of the 'wild animals,' which were arranged around the rotunda and aligned in a circle on a raised podium set at a twenty-five-degree angle. The cars were also behind protective nets, as it was out of the question that spectators touch them." At the entrance to the canvas pyramid, an extension played host to not one but three Ferrari 250 GTOs, the ultimate standard in Gran Turismo, of which only thirty-six examples were produced.

Before installing artworks, they had to be secured on loan. For *Tribute to Ferrari*, it was necessary to convince and negotiate. The Fondation Cartier joined forces with experts including Hervé Poulain and journalist Antoine Prunet. Another strong ally was Enzo Ferrari himself. In 1982, and despite having recently been made an honorary citizen of Fiorano,[11] the town in Italy neighboring Maranello, he declared that "the real Ferrari museum is now in France with Mr. Bardinon, who owns fifty-six of the

Fig 13 Three Ferrari GTO (1962–64) from the collection of Pierre Bardinon, at the Mas du Clos.

11. The test track of Scuderia Ferrari is located in the commune of Fiorano, bordering on Maranello. The circuit, measuring around three kilometers, was inaugurated on April 8, 1972.

Fig 14

Fig 15

Fig 14 and 15 Views of the installation of the exhibition, May 1987, Pierre Bardinon's collection.

12. Article published in the Italian magazine *Autosprint* in 1982.
13. Interview given to *Sport Auto* magazine in July 2003.
14. Johnny Rives (b. 1936), a friend of Claude Vialard also close to Pierre Bardinon, was the main writer on Formula 1 at the daily sports newspaper *L'Équipe* from the late 1960s up until 1996.

cars that I built.... I've often been forced to sell race-winning cars to pay my workers. I'm not ashamed to say that my wife also gave up her small gold dowry, a wedding gift from her parents, to pay my employees. You have to understand that under these conditions I haven't been able to afford to keep hold of any cars for a museum that might have become a testimony to my work."[12] Pierre Bardinon took over that role from Ferrari with remarkable foresight and intuition. "He was a precursor," says Emmanuel Zurini, a photographer and sculptor who knew Bardinon well. "Everything that was red, came from Maranello, and could be salvaged was for Pierre." Yet initially, the industrialist who made his fortune in leather and fur had set his sights on collecting Bugatti, Jaguar, Maserati, and Talbot. "The first Ferrari I owned was in 1961 or 1962: the 375 Plus from Le Mans in 1954, which won with [Maurice] Trintignant and [José Froilán] González," Pierre Bardinon told *Sport Auto* magazine in 2003.[13] "I was at Le Mans that year for the last or almost last time. I remember the emotion that I felt watching that car speed by. I would have been completely stunned if you'd told me that a few years later that very car would be mine. I had a taste for collecting, but not for archives and chassis numbers. So I asked Johnny Rives[14] to find me someone, a real historian, who could advise me. He pointed me in the direction of Claude Vialard, with whom I put the collection together. What I loved about the cars above all were the forms, which is why I had so few Formula 1 cars." Claude Vialard first became fascinated by the cars from Maranello as a young boy. He would buy stacks of magazines, from which he would cut out technical spec sheets and articles detailing the victories of each Italian race car. This long-term car culture later allowed him to become Bardinon's mentor. "Pierre asked me what I saw as the collection's soul," says Vialard. "I instinctively replied, 'Cars with race victories.' So he got rid of the 'customer' cars as they were known and any other modified ones that he owned. The heart of the collection revolved around thirty race cars. You have to bear in mind that those cars from the 1950s and 1960s, including certain unique cars built specifically for races like

Gentile signor Bardinon,

il presidente della Cartier,
in una sua recente visita a Maranello, mi ha parlato
della iniziativa che la "fondation Cartier" intrapren-
dera' nei prossimi mesi.

Credo che il suo aiuto e piu' in particolare l'esposi-
zione di alcune delle sue belle Ferrari possa contri-
buire alla migliore riuscita della iniziativa, alla
quale fin da ora auguro il migliore successo.

Cordiali saluti,

Gent.mo signor
PIERRE BARDINON
Le Mas Du Clos
Les Puids
23200 AUBUSSON
France

Modena, 9 dicembre 1986

Fig 16

the 24 Hours of Le Mans, Mille Miglia, and Targa Florio, were genuine works of art—and Pierre was flattered that the Fondation Cartier asked to borrow them for the exhibition." Others were suggesting working with the collection including Jean Todt, Hervé Poulain, who both appreciated the value of unveiling so many beautiful cars and their legendary numbers—250 MM, 375 Plus, 275 P, 330 P, 412 P, 512 M, 312 P—and most importantly, Enzo Ferrari himself. "Enzo picked up the phone to call Bardinon in front of me," said Alain Dominique Perrin, "and I know that he followed up with a letter." That letter, dated December 9, 1986, would prove an immense help:

Fig 16 Letter from Enzo Ferrari to Pierre Bardinon, December 9, 1986.

Fig 17

Fig 18

Fig 17 and 18 Views of the installation of the exhibition, May 1987, Pierre Bardinon's collection.

"Dear Mr. Bardinon,

The president of Cartier, during a recent visit to Maranello, spoke to me of the initiative that the 'Fondation Cartier' will undertake in the next few months. I believe that your help, and more specifically the exhibition of some of your beautiful Ferraris, could contribute to the success of this initiative, to which I already wish the greatest success.

Yours sincerely,

Enzo Ferrari."

The collection of the Association du Mas du Clos—the name under which Pierre Bardinon's cars were presented—would become the jewel at the heart of the *Tribute to Ferrari* exhibition. Shown beneath the pyramid designed by Andrée Putman, twenty-three of the Prancing Horse's most prestigious models sparkled on silver-leather-covered podiums. "Pierre had made his own selection, and I didn't get involved," recalls Claude Vialard. "On the other hand, he didn't know how to present them, but then the layout came to me suddenly. In the days leading up to the opening, I checked that everything was in line with what we had suggested to the scenographers. I also took care of the technical spec sheets for each model." These sheets were used to put together the information labels for the cars, which were supplemented by illustrated panels telling the story of Ferrari from 1947.

At the entrance to Domaine du Montcel, in the area named the "Village," Marie-Claude Beaud had to knock down the walls of a building to get the prototypes and scale-one models inside. The fourth chapter of this life-sized story opened with "La Mécanique et le design" (Mechanics and Design), which sketched the glory days of the close relationship between Enzo Ferrari and Gian-Battista Pinin Farina, two twentieth-century Italian geniuses who united their talents, beginning in 1951. Sigma, Zaz, and Modulo—some of the esoteric names for unique models with incongruous designs that the pair imagined—were surrounded by a Testarossa prototype and blueprint drawings from the Pininfarina archives framed and hung on the walls. Some of the mightiest powertrains ever produced

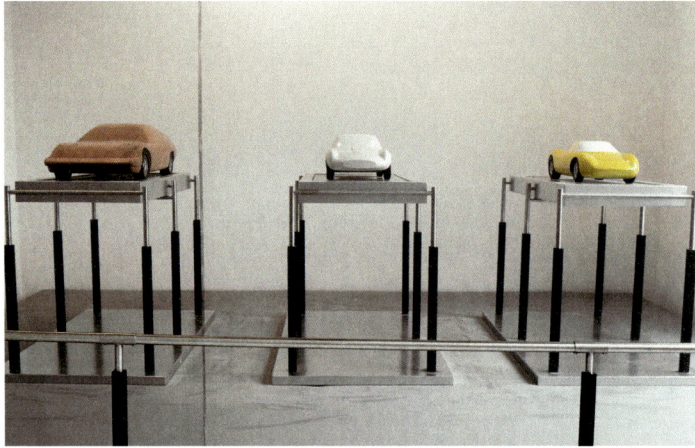

Fig 19   Fig 20

in the workshops of Maranello were on show. Moinard designed the displays that showcased them, and found a wrinkle paint, similar to the paint used on the valve covers of V12 engines, to finish the legs. Rather than hearing the characteristic roar of Ferrari engines, visitors were treated to an immersive sound installation in one room that allowed them to experience the mechanical world of racing and the atmosphere of Formula 1 circuits. "We worked with a group specialized in minimalist music," says Beaud. "Everything matters in an exhibition: appearance, color, technical details, and also sound. Particularly since the sound of a Ferrari is a genuine invention." The "Village" also welcomed the results of the Fondation's commissions for ten photographers: Alain Bizos, Agnès Bonnot, Pierre-Olivier Deschamps, Pascal Dolémieux and Xavier Lambours from Agence VU', François Le Diascorn of the Rapho agency, Franco Fontana, Frank Horvat, Erica Lennard, and Jeanloup Sieff. Christian Caujolle, the head of Agence VU' and a long-time friend of Marie-Claude Beaud, coordinated the project. An eleventh photographer was supposed to have been part of the commission: Guy Bourdin. "He accepted in principle to take a series of photos of Ferraris and models," says Christian Caujolle. "The shoot was supposed to happen in Étretat, in Normandy. Everyone arrived at the location—the cars, the models—but Bourdin never showed."

Other photographers went to Mulhouse, Berne, Turin, Modena, and to the racetracks of Jacarepaguá in Rio de Janeiro and Imola—officially named the Autodromo Internazionale Enzo e Dino Ferrari—as well as Jacky Setton's track in Crespières, just outside Paris, and Pierre Bardinon's in Saint-Avit-de-Tardes in the Creuse in central France. Not forgetting Maranello, obviously. Jeanloup Sieff was supposed to take Enzo Ferrari's portrait, but broke his leg and was replaced at the last minute by Pierre-Olivier Deschamps. "A moment like that is always memorable," he says. "The shoot took place in Enzo Ferrari's office; he never moved from his leather armchair. I spoke to him in Italian and slightly naively confessed that it was a great honor to meet him. His only reply was that he had a very common name. This felt like proof that he still had a keen sense of

Fig 19 and 20 View of the exhibition spaces of the "Village" where smaller models, preparatory drawings, and a prototype model of Testarossa were presented (1981).

Fig 21 Valerio Adami, *Mars-avril 1987, Monaco*, 1987, acrylic paint on canvas, 198 × 147.5 cm. Commission from the Fondation Cartier pour l'art contemporain for the *Tribute to Ferrari* exhibition.

AN EXHIBITION AHEAD OF ITS TIME

Fig 22

Fig 22 Contact print of a series of photographs of Enzo Ferrari taken by Pierre-Olivier Deschamps in Maranello in April 1987, commissioned by the Fondation Cartier pour l'art contemporain for the *Tribute to Ferrari* exhibition.

Fig 23

Fig 24

Fig 23 and 24 View of the exhibition
spaces of the "Village," where the
photographs taken by the ten
commissioned photographers were
shown.

his modest origins, even though he was the head of one of the world's
most prestigious firms. The session lasted fifteen to twenty minutes. I
used a 6 × 6 Hasselblad and an open flash, as many of my colleagues did
at the time. Enzo Ferrari was wearing a white shirt with a vest, a tie, and
a light-colored suit. There's the shadow of his profile on the right-hand
side, which was an effect created by the flash, but it's possible that the
sun shining through the window reflected some light. I took only one roll
of twelve shots." Shot in April 1987, one month before *Tribute to Ferrari*
opened, this portrait was the only photograph of Enzo Ferrari taken for
the Fondation Cartier exhibition.

Installing the exhibition felt like a non-stop ballet, during which trans-
porters, mechanics, Bruno Moinard and the technicians from the design
studio, and Marie-Claude Beaud's team, including Hervé Chandès, who
had just been hired and would succeed her as head of the Fondation
Carter thirteen years later, all crossed paths. "While we didn't take deliv-
ery of all the cars in one go, there was very little time between each one's
arrival," says Beaud. "Pierre Bardinon and Jack Setton were not there all
the time, and what stunned me during the set-up was the precision of the
gestures of their assistants and mechanics."

A storm broke over Jouy-en-Josas the night before the opening.
Bruno was horrified to see "the balloons on the ground," but in an Italian
miracle, on Friday May 22, 1987, everything was in place and the exhibition *Tribute to Ferrari* was inaugurated, under a leaden sky, by Alain
Dominique Perrin, Marie-Claude Beaud, and Piero Ferrari.[15] His father
Enzo did not travel, as expected. Since his first son, Dino, had died aged
twenty-four of muscular dystrophy, Enzo Ferrari had sworn never to
leave Maranello. During the opening, Piero Ferrari read a transcribed
message from his father, recorded a few weeks earlier in a short video
in which the Commendatore expressed his joy about the exhibition
and wished it great success. "It was a truly spectacular event," remembers Piero Ferrari. "Suspended by parachutes, our cars seemed to float;
they transformed the park into this magical place. When I got back, my

15. Piero Ferrari (b. 1945) is currently
vice-chair of Ferrari.

AN EXHIBITION AHEAD OF ITS TIME

  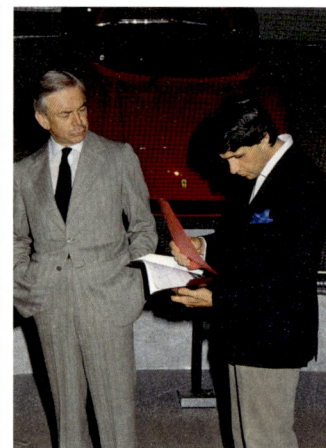

father asked me a lot of questions: he wanted to know how the cars had been exhibited, who was at the show, what my impressions were. There were modern cars next to the magnificent classics that had made our company's name. It was so exciting to see our cars treated as works of art at a time when that was still not the case. I remember at a certain moment finding myself on stage with Alain Prost. He had already won two world championships with McLaren.[16] We exchanged a few words, joking around. I had the chance to speak to him at greater length three years later, when he became one of our two Formula 1 drivers." An odd coincidence, indeed. (In 1990, Alain Prost was hired by the Scuderia to cross swords with his ex-teammate, Brazilian driver Ayrton Senna.)

Also present was Jean Todt, an old friend of Alain Dominique Perrin and close to Pierre Bardinon. In January 1987, the team he led, Peugeot Talbot Sport, won the Paris–Dakar Rally for the first time with a Peugeot 205 Turbo 16 Grand Raid. Six years later, Todt would be named head of sport at Ferrari, a first for a Frenchman. Certain French political figures were also in attendance: future prime minister Édith Cresson, minister of culture François Léotard, and minister of health Michèle Barzach all greeted Alain Dominique Perrin and his guests, notably Andrée Putman (who had designed a desk for previous culture minister Jack Lang). Numerous journalists, both French and Italian, were also there. Yves Mourousi presented the lunchtime news on TF1, the most popular French network, live from Jouy-en-Josas. César chatted with Keith Haring, the star of street art. Jack Setton talked with Bernard Arnault. François Le Diascorn photographed the guests.

Monique Le Saint, the mayor of Jouy-en-Josas was overjoyed to witness the invasion of gleaming star cars. The impact on the town was considerable, and her constituents soon lost count of the number of Ferraris parked in the streets around the Domaine du Montcel.

Two weeks later, on June 6, 7, and 8, this high society was invited to three dinners hosted by the Fondation Cartier. Christine Borgoltz, then head of PR at the Fondation and mistress of ceremonies, drew up the

Fig 25, 26 and 27 Piero Ferrari, Alain Prost, Jack Setton, Yves Mourousi, and Alain Dominique Perrin (1), Jean Todt and César (2), Pierre Bardinon and Jack Setton (3), at the opening events of the exhibition.

16. Alain Prost (b. 1955) won fifty-one Grand Prix races and was the Formula 1 drivers' world champion in 1985, 1986, and 1989 with McLaren Racing. In 1990, he joined Scuderia Ferrari, for which he competed in thirty Grands Prix, garnering five victories. He won a fourth world title in 1993, with Williams Racing.

Fig 28

Fig 29

Fig 28 Andrée Putman during the exhibition opening.

Fig 29 Exhibition opening.

17. The original version of Enzo Ferrari's autobiography, *Le mie gioie terribile* (My terrible joys) was published in 1962 (Cappelli Editions, Bologna). The fourth chapter, entitled "Piloti, che gente…" (Drivers, what people…), was augmented and modernized in its new version, the French version of which was published in 1987 on the occasion of the *Tribute to Ferrari* exhibition, co-published with E.P.A. Publishers.
18. Valerio Adami (b. 1935) divided his time between France and Italy. In the seventies, he was one of the representatives of New Figuration. His work was the subject of a major retrospective at the Centre Pompidou in 1985.

guest list with the help of Jean Todt and Andrée Putman. An exhibition in homage to Ferrari had to have Italian food, so the Faiola brothers, who had bought Stresa, a restaurant in the eighth arrondissement of Paris, and who were friends with César, were put in charge of the menu.

The public rushed to Jouy-en-Josas. They were assisted during their visit by some fifteen hostesses and guides, all dressed in red overalls, most of them students selected from the surrounding Yvelines département. They handed out a booklet containing a map of the park, a chronology and list of championships won by Ferrari, and a glossary to help visitors understand the technical differences between the models on show. Above all, the guides were there to ensure that people remained at a safe distance from the cars. "What surprised and delighted us was how visitors would stay for hours and hours in the park," recalls Christine Borgoltz. "At weekends, it was always full." The visitor experience, that cost 35 Francs at that time, would often finish with a visit to the gift store next to the café, where Ferrari-branded key rings, umbrellas, badges, baseball caps, 1/43-scale models, watches, and pens were available, accompanied by car magazines, books, including *Piloti, che gente…*, a translated version of Enzo Ferrari's autobiography,[17] and finally, a lithograph by Franco-Italian painter Valerio Adami.[18]

On July 10, 1987, the AFP news agency published the following item: "*Tribute to Ferrari*, the exhibition featuring forty-five vehicles from the great Italian automaker, at the Fondation Cartier in Jouy-en-Josas, will be extended until August 30, the Fondation announced on Friday. Alain Dominique Perrin, president of Cartier International, took the decision in light of the enormous success of the exhibition, which opened on May 22 and was originally set to close on July 26." Despite some criticism, essentially from the contemporary art world—which saw certain people label the Fondation Cartier's president a "garage mechanic"—and thanks to the numerous articles in both the general and specialist press, more than ninety thousand people came to admire the Ferraris. "It was a turning point in the history of the Fondation Cartier," says Marie-Claude

Fig 30

Beaud. For the man behind the retrospective, Alain Dominique Perrin, it was "*the* turning point." *Tribute to Ferrari* was put together at 300 kmph (200 mph), leaving no time to produce a catalogue. Thirty-eight years later, this book is not only a richly deserved homage to this prestigious carmaker—but also pays tribute to an exhibition that became legendary.

This text was written in January 2025 based on interviews by Philippe Séclier held from September to December 2024 with Piero Ferrari, Alain Dominique Perrin, Marie-Claude Beaud, Christine Borgoltz, Bruno Moinard, Jack Setton, Daniel Marin, Hervé Poulain, Claude Vialard, Christian Caujolle, Pierre-Olivier Deschamps, and Emmanuel Zurini.

Fig 30 View of the park of the Fondation Cartier, May 22, 1987.

Opposite and following pages:
Bruno Moinard, *Tribute to Ferrari*, markers and ink on paper, 20 × 30 cm, 2024.

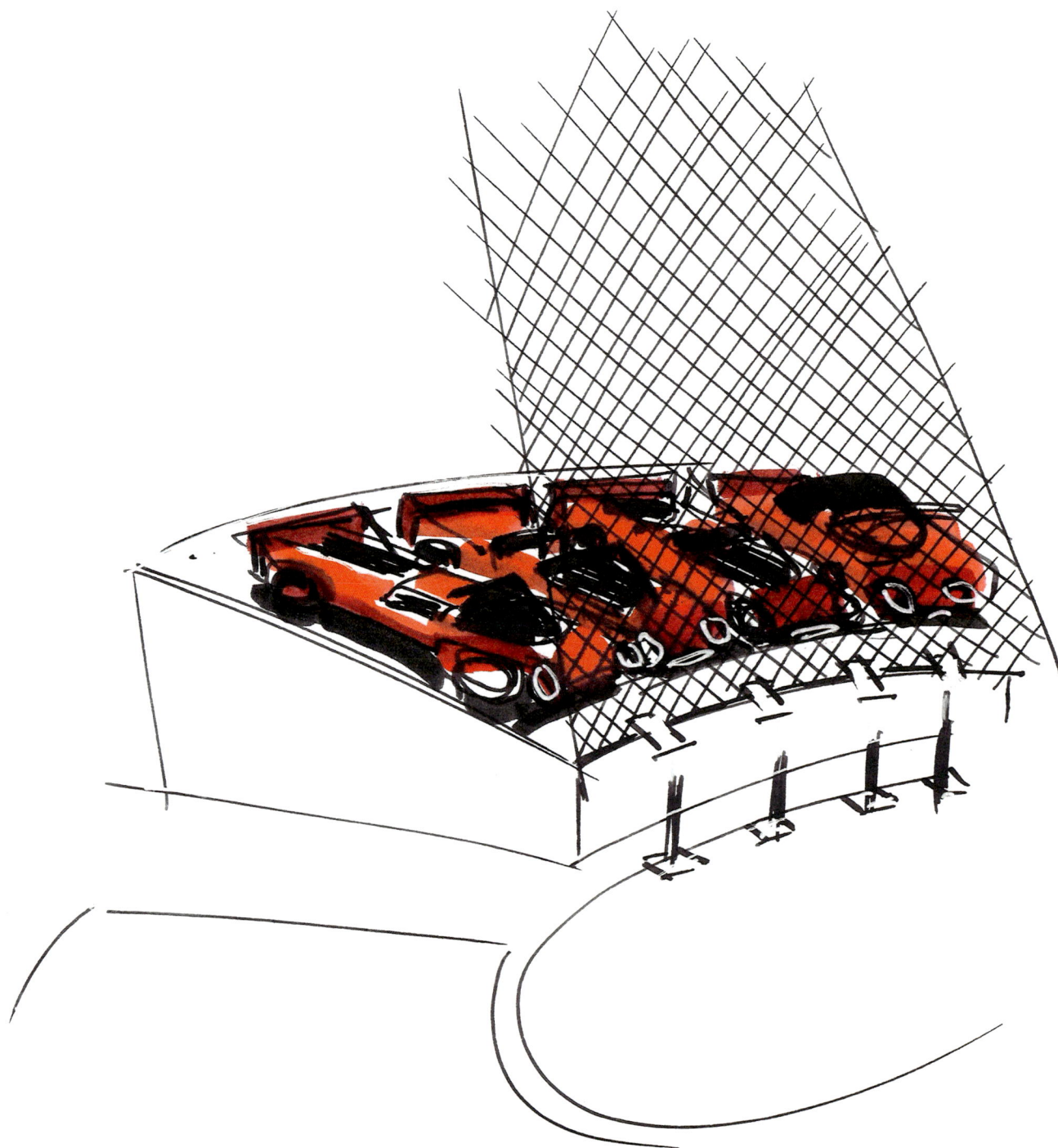

1

ferrari

FONDATION Cartier

◇ HOMMAGE A FERRARI ◇
22 MAI ◇ 26 JUILLET 1987

④
VILLAGE
◇ FERRARI ◇ PININFARINA ◇
LA MÉCANIQUE ET LE DESIGN

- SIGMA PROTOTYPE 1963
- FORMULE 1 "ZAZ" PROTOTYPE 1979
- P 6 AVEC SA DÉCLINAISON 1969
- MODÈLE PROTOTYPE TESTAROSSA 198
- 512 S MODULO 1970
- DINO 206 JAUNE 1967

◇ FERRARI ◇
COMMANDE A 10 PHOTOGRAPHES

ALAIN BIZOS
AGNÈS BONNOT
PIERRE OLIVIER DESCHAMPS
PASCAL DOLÉMIEUX
FRANCO FONTANA
FRANK HORVAT
XAVIER LAMBOURS
FRANÇOIS LE DIASCORN
ERICA LENNARD
JEAN LOUP SIEFF

①
PYRAMIDE
◇ FERRARI ◇
HISTOIRE ET LÉGENDE

• 250 MM	1953	• 412 P	1966/67	
• 375 MM	1953	• 330 P4	1967	
• 375 •	1954	• 312 P	1969	
• 410 COUPÉ	1955	• 512 M	1970/71	
• 410 S	1955		◇	
• 290 MM	1956			
• 335 S	1957	• 166 CORSA	1950	
• 250 TR	1958	• 250 GTO	1962	
• DINO 246 S	1960	• 250 GTO	1963	
• 330 TR LM	1962	• 250 GTO	1964	
• 268 SP	1962	• 365 P	1964 • CHASSIS	
• 275 P	1963	• 312 S	1970	
• 330 P	1964	• 312 PB	1972	

②
PARC
◇ FERRARI ◇
LA ROUTE
BERLINETTES ET CABRIOLETS

- • MONDIAL CABRIOLET 1982
- • 365 GTC 1971
- • 512 BB 1976
- • 378 GTS 1985
- • DINO 246 GT 1973
- • 288 GTO 1984
- • TESTAROSSA 1984
- • 412 1985
- • DAYTONA 1971
- • 212 INTER 1952
- • SUPER AMERICA 1962

③
BUNKER
◇ FERRARI ◇
LE MONDE DE LA COURSE
MONOPLACES

• 312 F1 1968	
312 B2 1971	
312 T 1975	
312 T3 1978	
312 T4 1979	
• 625 F1 1955	
156 1966	
1512 1965	
212 E 1969	

RUE ADANSON

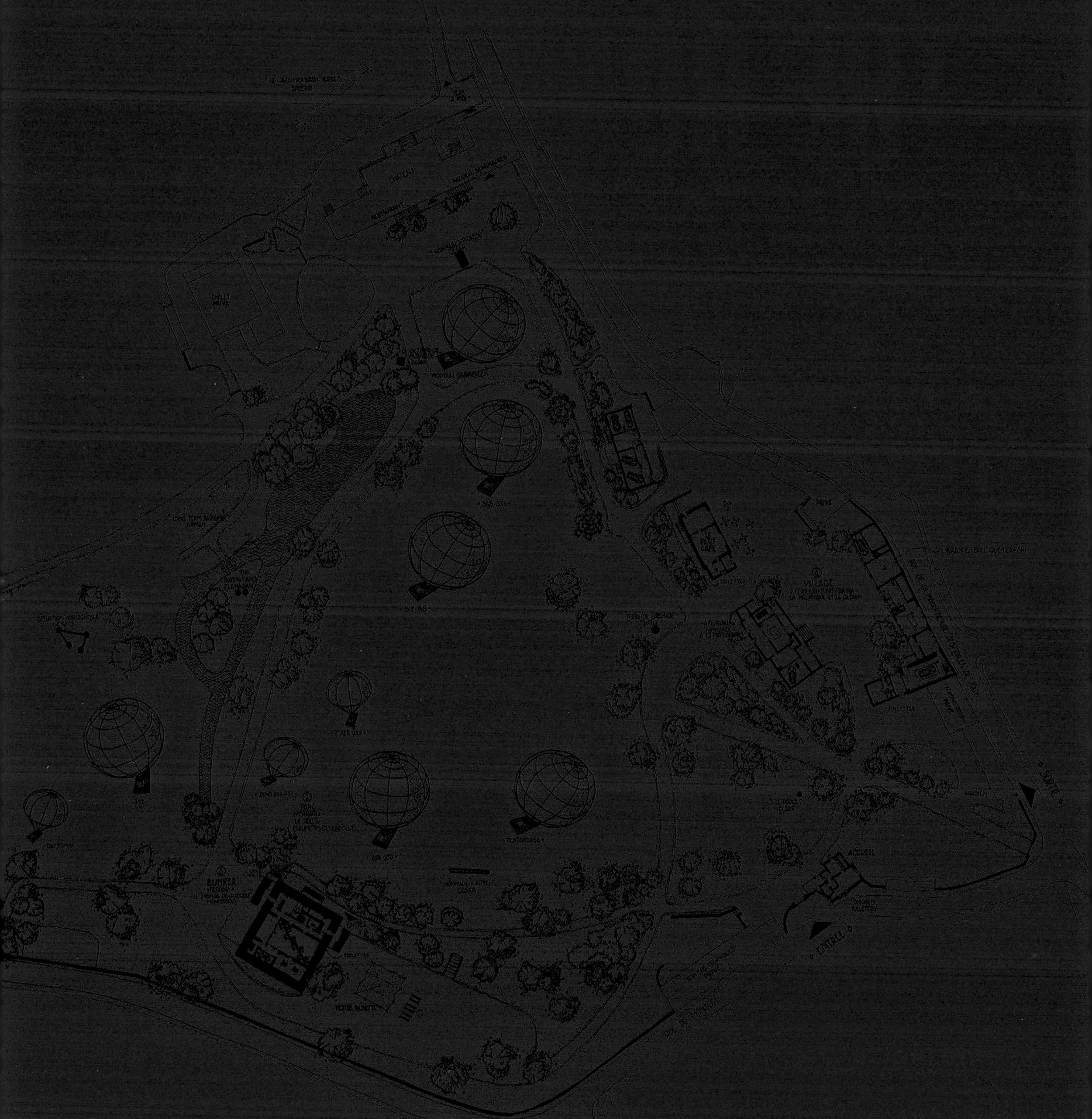
VILLAGE
BUNKER
ACCUEIL
SORTIE
ENTREE

THE ROAD

THIS COLOR AND ME

Andrée Putman

Designer, scenographer of the exhibition

This color and me, we thought we had seen red with each other! Because to handle this shade properly demands conditions that are difficult to bring together. I was stuck using homeopathic doses, like the red line on a cotton crêpe bandage. What this color triggered in me was shyness— even stage fright—more than displeasure. Today I go red at my mistake... As a shy colorist, I was probably waiting for the right moment, the right opportunity to tackle it, a project that would come naturally and lead me to see red one fine morning! As for cars, they and I also have a difficult past. We had treated each other badly. Holding on to the magic they convey, mentally unable to "lift the hood," a mystery not to be revealed and one I had never tried to pierce. Ironic, then, to be asked to think about the installation and presentation of red cars. Followed by a feeling of confusion to be among the chosen ones. Was it a mistake? A paranoia that carried its own share of luck. Always remember that every error, catastrophe, or absurdity also carries a positive seed. Speaking of the positive, and if we must talk about it, the ingredients at the Fondation Cartier were the most beautiful cars in the world, the desire to surpass ourselves to honor Mr. Ferrari, and an admirable park.

After that, it's easy to understand. We, the directors of this extravaganza, had been given something to dream about. Stunned by the enormity and poetry of the adventure, we laughed, and freed from the duty of being too serious, we were able to face these admirable objects. Weren't these cars just toys and the human beings children? So we set about accounting for our dreams. The cars would come down "from heaven," transported at night, dropped into place by hot-air balloon and parachute, delivered at dawn in the dew of the park, then arranged, some under cover. Sometimes at night, a Technicolor nightmare assailed me, always the same one: gleaming red (the cars) and green (the park) under the horrified gaze of collectors and the public the cars would leave, one by one, and we would lose them from sight high up in a *Babar*-like, sapphire-blue sky, behind the final curtain of cumulonimbus clouds! PARIS, 1987

Pages 46–47: General exhibition plan distributed to visitors, 1987.

Above and following pages: Views of the *Tribute to Ferrari* exhibition, 1987
Testarossa (1984), 288 GTO (1984)
In the background: Jean Pierre Raynaud, *La Serre* and *Pot Doré* (1985)

512 BB (1976)

Daytona (1971), 512 BB (1976), 288 GTO (1984), 328 GTS (1985)

512 BB (1976)

412 (1985) and 330 GTC (1966)

Dino 246 GT (1973)

Pages 61–68: Preparatory drawings made by Bruno Moinard for Andrée Putman's scenography, October 1986

Ferrari

ECART
111 RUE ST ANTOINE
PARIS 1er OCT. 86

FONDATION
Cartier

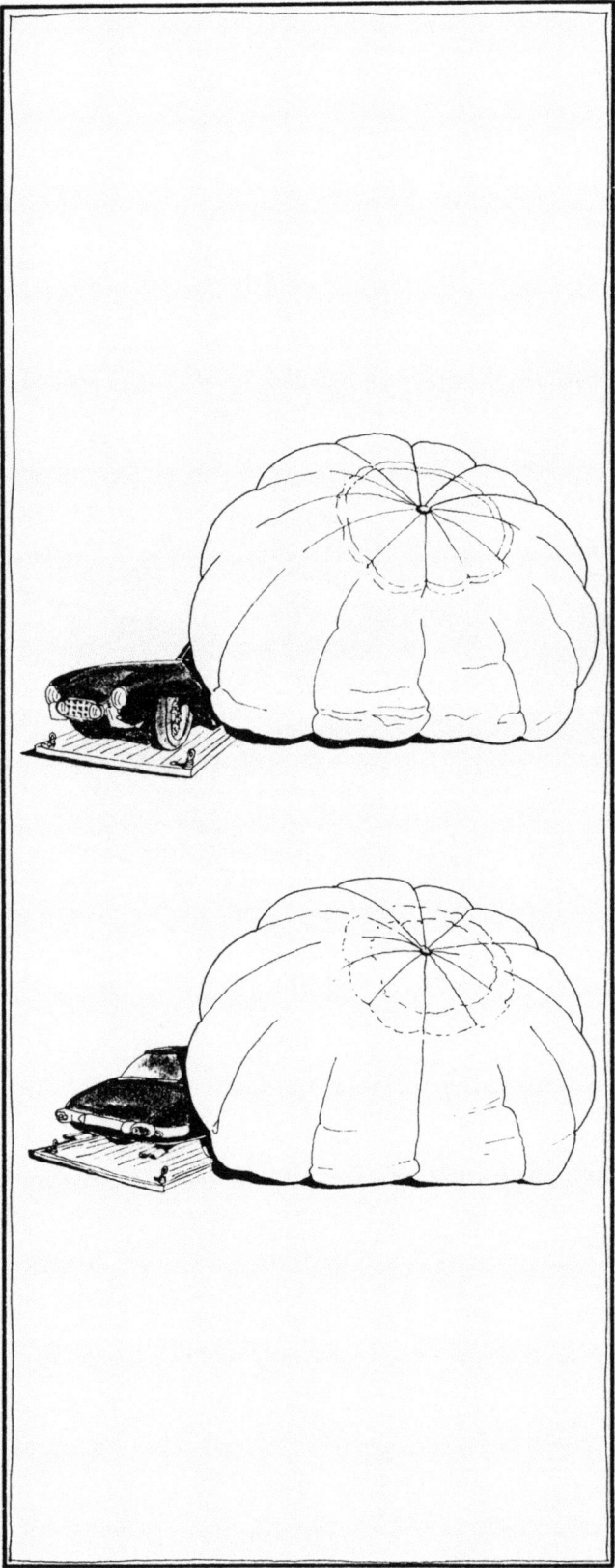

Above and following pages: Views of the *Tribute to Ferrari* exhibition, 1987
Daytona (1971)

Mondial Cabriolet (1982), Daytona (1971), 512 BB (1976), and Testarossa (1984)
In the background: César, *Hommage à Eiffel* (1991)

512 BB (1976)

512 BB (1976)

Testarossa (1984) and 288 GTO (1984)

Testarossa (1984) and 412 (1985)

212 Inter (1952)

2

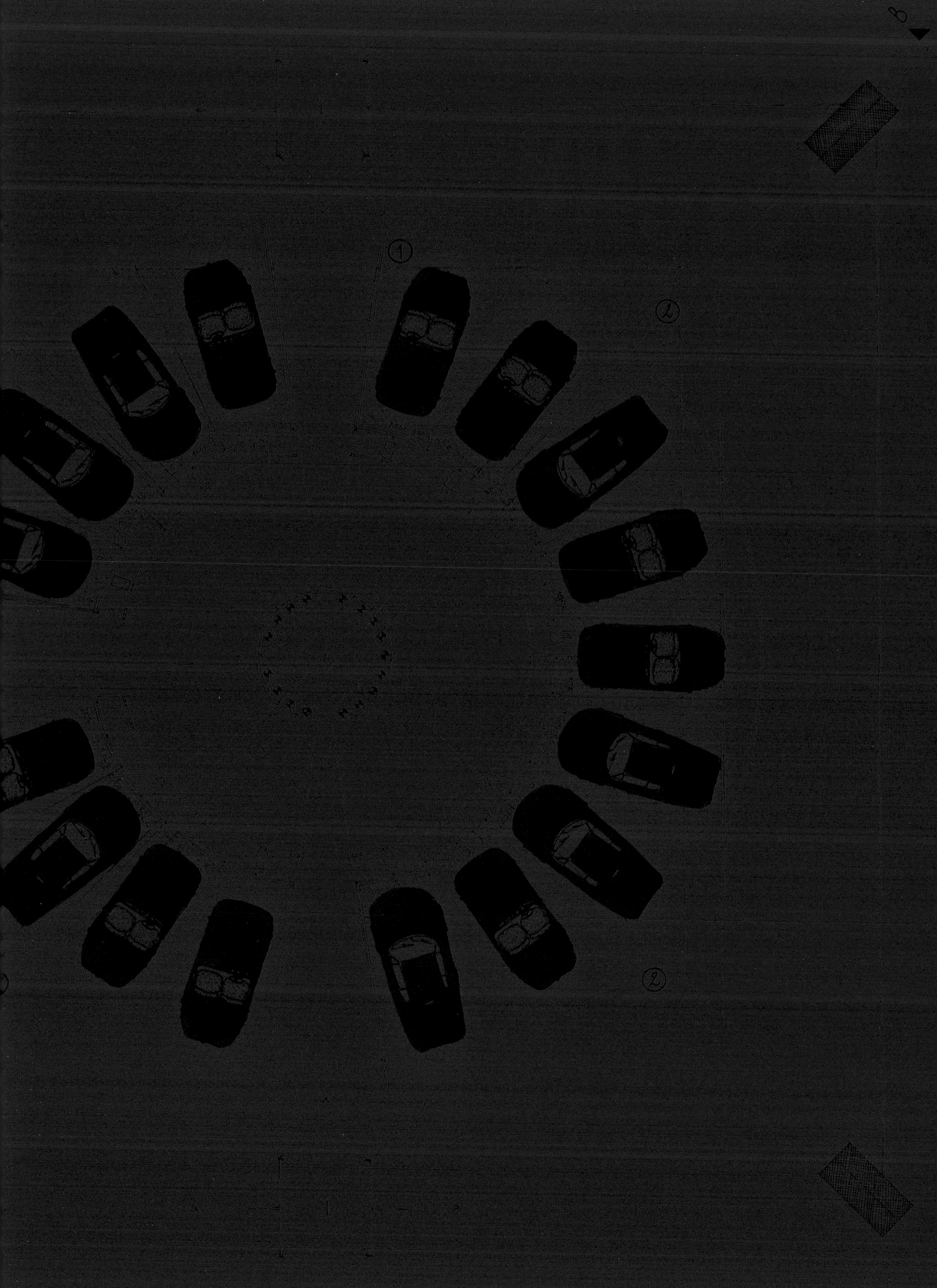
1
2
2

HISTORY
AND LEGEND

PIERRE BARDINON'S MAS DU CLOS COLLECTION

The mechanical masterpieces belonging to Pierre Bardinon (1931–2012) were presented under the great pyramid installed in the center of the Fondation Cartier's park, and proved one of the exhibition's high points. A business leader and entrepreneur from the Creuse region of central France where his family had founded a tannery in the nineteenth century, Bardinon had been collecting cars since the 1960s and had built a race track at his home, Château du Mas du Clos in Saint-Avit-de-Tardes in the Creuse, where renowned drivers and prestigious teams would come to practice. It was there that the legend of the Association du Mas du Clos and its unique collection of Ferraris was born. At the time of the exhibition, Bardinon owned fifty-six cars bearing the *cavallino rampante* (Prancing Horse), of which twenty-three were selected for the exhibition. Their excellent condition (thanks to the meticulous work of Modena-based coachbuilder Fiorenzo Fantuzzi), rarity, and remarkable track records (four of them had won the 24 Hours of Le Mans) made them exceptional. They were all sports cars, sports prototypes, or Gran Turismo, with two exceptions: a 166 Corsa, with its front-mounted engine, driven by Franco Cortese in 1950, and a 312 B in which Jacky Ickx won three Grands Prix in 1970. Unfortunately, Pierre Bardinon's collection was split up during the 2010s.

Pages 82–83: Installation plan for the cars of the Mas du Clos Collection, 1987.

Above and following pages: Views of the *Tribute to Ferrari* exhibition, 1987

From left to right:
275 P (1963), 330 P (1964), 412 P (1967), 330 P4 (1967), 312 P (1969), 512 M (1970)

412 P (1967), 330 P4 (1967), 312 P (1969), 512 M (1970), 250 MM (1953), 375 MM (1953), 375 Plus (1954), 410 S (1955)

250 MM (1953), 375 MM (1953), 375 Plus (1954), 410 S (1955), 410 CM (1955), 290 MM (1956), 335 S (1957)

250 MM (1953), 375 MM (1953), 375 Plus (1954)

410 S (1955), 410 CM (1955), 290 MM (1956)

412 P (1967), 330 P4 (1967), 312 P (1969), 512 M (1970)

1970-71

COLLECTION MAS DU CLOS

335 S (1957), 250 TR (1958), DINO 246 S (1960)

330 TRI LM (1962), 268 SP (1962), 275 P (1963), 330 P (1964)

312 P (1972), 365 P (chassis), 312 B (1969) (background)

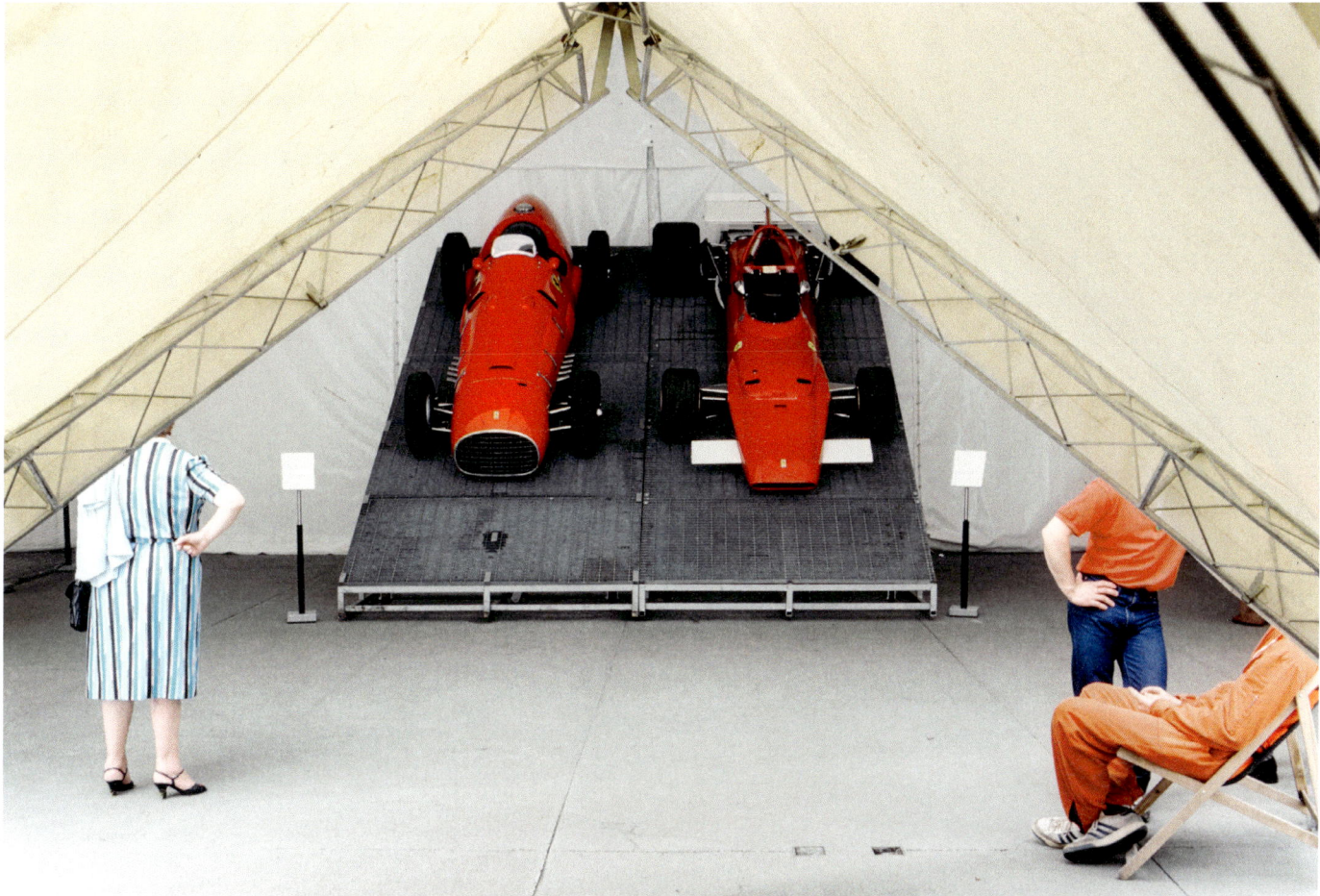

166 Corsa (1950), 312 B (1969)

166 Corsa (1950)

166 CORSA

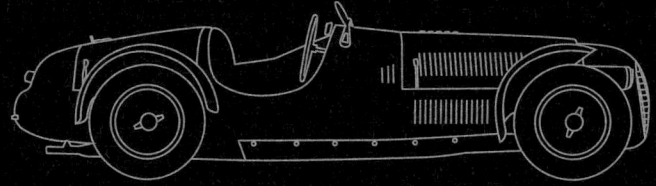

PRODUCTION

YEAR OF PRODUCTION	1950
CHASSIS NUMBER	#006C

ENGINE

TYPE	V12 at 60° (front longitudinal)
ENGINE SIZE	1,995.02 cm^3 (60 × 58.8 mm)
MAXIMUM POWER	155 hp at 7,000 rpm
DISTRIBUTION	1 camshaft, 2 spark plugs per cylinder
FUEL FEED	3 Weber 32 DCF carburetors

CHASSIS

FRAME	Tubular steel
GEARBOX	5 gears and reverse

BODYWORK

TYPE	1-seater F2
WHEELBASE	216 cm
TRACK WIDTH	120 cm at the front and rear
WEIGHT (EMPTY)	550 kg

PALMARES

Franco Cortese's personal car

250 MM

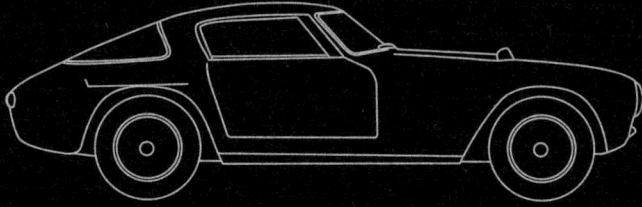

PRODUCTION

YEAR OF PRODUCTION	1953
CHASSIS NUMBER	#0344 MM

ENGINE

TYPE	V12 at 60° (front longitudinal)
ENGINE SIZE	2,953.21 cm³ (73 × 58.8 mm)
MAXIMUM POWER	240 hp at 7,200 rpm
DISTRIBUTION	1 camshaft, 2 spark plugs per cylinder
FUEL FEED	3 Weber 36 IF/4C carburetors

CHASSIS

FRAME	Tubular steel
GEARBOX	4 gears and reverse

BODYWORK

DESIGNER	Pininfarina
TYPE	2-seater Berlinetta
WHEELBASE	240 cm
TRACK WIDTH	130 cm at the front, 132 cm at the rear
WEIGHT (EMPTY)	900 kg

375 MM

PRODUCTION

YEAR OF PRODUCTION	1953
CHASSIS NUMBER	#0368AM

ENGINE

TYPE	V12 at 60° (front longitudinal)
ENGINE SIZE	4,522.68 cm³ (84 × 68 mm)
MAXIMUM POWER	340 hp at 7,000 rpm
DISTRIBUTION	1 camshaft, 2 spark plugs per cylinder
FUEL FEED	3 Weber 40 IF/4C carburetors

CHASSIS

FRAME	Tubular steel
GEARBOX	4 gears and reverse

BODYWORK

DESIGNER	Pininfarina
TYPE	2-seater Berlinetta
WHEELBASE	260 cm
TRACK WIDTH	132.5 cm at the front, 132 cm at the rear
WEIGHT (EMPTY)	900 kg

PALMARES

Champion of the 1953 World Sports Car Championship

375 PLUS

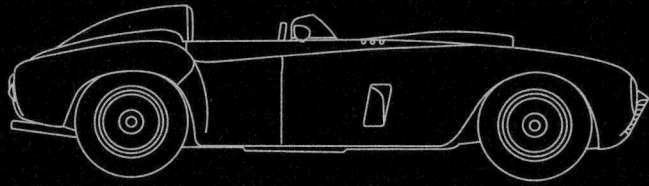

PRODUCTION

YEAR OF PRODUCTION	1954
CHASSIS NUMBER	#0396 AM

ENGINE

TYPE	V12 at 60° (front longitudinal)
ENGINE SIZE	4,954.34 cm^3 (84 × 74.5 mm)
MAXIMUM POWER	330 hp at 6,000 rpm
DISTRIBUTION	1 camshaft, 2 spark plugs per cylinder
FUEL FEED	3 Weber 46 DCF/3 carburetors

CHASSIS

FRAME	Tubular steel
GEARBOX	5 gears and reverse

BODYWORK

DESIGNER	Pininfarina
TYPE	2-seater Spider
WHEELBASE	260 cm
TRACK WIDTH	132.5 cm at the front, 128.4 cm at the rear
WEIGHT (EMPTY)	1,030 kg

PALMARES

JOSÉ FROILÁN GONZÁLEZ AND MAURICE TRINTIGNANT
First, 24 Hours of Le Mans, France,
June 12–13, 1954

Champion of the 1954 World Sports Car
Championship

410 S

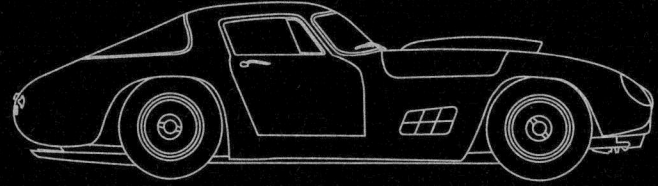

PRODUCTION

YEAR OF PRODUCTION	1955
CHASSIS NUMBER	#0594 CM

ENGINE

TYPE	V12 at 60° (front longitudinal)
ENGINE SIZE	4,962.96 cm^3 (88 × 68 mm)
MAXIMUM POWER	340 hp at 6,200 rpm
DISTRIBUTION	1 camshaft, 2 spark plugs per cylinder
FUEL FEED	3 Weber 42 DCZ/3 carburetors

CHASSIS

FRAME	Tubular steel
GEARBOX	5 gears and reverse

BODYWORK

DESIGNER	Scaglietti
TYPE	2-seater Berlinetta
WHEELBASE	242 cm
TRACK WIDTH	145.5 cm at the front, 145 cm at the rear
WEIGHT (EMPTY)	1,200 kg

410 CM

PRODUCTION

YEAR OF PRODUCTION	1955
CHASSIS NUMBER	#0596 CM

ENGINE

TYPE	V12 at 60° (front longitudinal)
ENGINE SIZE	4,962.96 cm³ (84 × 68 mm)
MAXIMUM POWER	340 hp at 6 200 rpm
DISTRIBUTION	1 camshaft, 2 spark plugs per cylinder
FUEL FEED	3 Weber 42 DCZ/3 carburetors

CHASSIS

FRAME	Tubular steel
GEARBOX	4 gears and reverse

BODYWORK

DESIGNER	Scaglietti
TYPE	2-seater Spider
WHEELBASE	242 cm
TRACK WIDTH	145.5 cm at the front, 145 cm at the rear
WEIGHT (EMPTY)	1,200 kg

290 MM

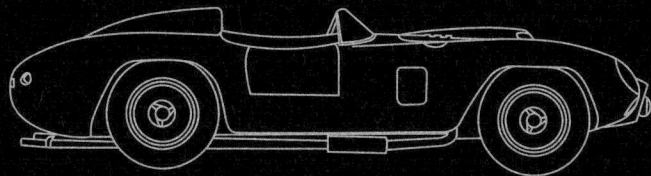

PRODUCTION

YEAR OF PRODUCTION	1956
CHASSIS NUMBER	#0626

ENGINE

TYPE	V12 at 60° (front longitudinal)
ENGINE SIZE	3,490.61 cm³ (73 × 69.5 mm)
MAXIMUM POWER	320 hp at 7,200 rpm
DISTRIBUTION	1 camshaft, 2 spark plugs per cylinder
FUEL FEED	3 Weber 36 IR4/C1 carburetors

CHASSIS

FRAME	Tubular steel
GEARBOX	4 gears and reverse

BODYWORK

DESIGNER	Scaglietti
TYPE	2-seater Spider
WHEELBASE	235 cm
TRACK WIDTH	129.6 cm at the front, 131 cm at the rear
WEIGHT (EMPTY)	880 kg

PALMARES

JUAN MANUEL FANGIO
Fourth, Mille Miglia, Italy, April 28—29, 1956
PHIL HILL AND KEN WHARTON
Third, 1,000 km of Nürburgring, Germany,
May 27, 1956
MASTEN GREGORY
Second, Portuguese Grand Prix, Boavista Monsanto
Park, June 9, 1957
PETER COLLINS AND WOLFGANG VON TRIPS
Second, Swedish Grand Prix, Kristianstad,
August 12, 1956
LUIGI MUSSO, EUGENIO CASTELLOTTI,
MASTEN GREGORY AND CESARE PERDISA
First, 1,000 km of Buenos Aires, Argentina,
January 20, 1957

Champion of the 1956 World Sports Car Championship

335 S

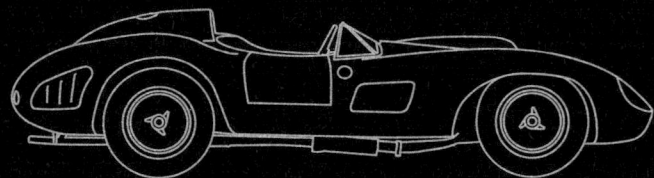

PRODUCTION

YEAR OF PRODUCTION	1957
CHASSIS NUMBER	#0674

ENGINE

TYPE	V12 at 60° (front longitudinal)
ENGINE SIZE	4,023.32 cm^3 (77 × 72 mm)
MAXIMUM POWER	390 hp at 7,400 rpm
DISTRIBUTION	1 camshaft, 2 spark plugs per cylinder
FUEL FEED	6 Weber 44 DCN carburetors

CHASSIS

FRAME	Tubular steel
GEARBOX	4 gears and reverse

BODYWORK

DESIGNER	Scaglietti
TYPE	2-seater Spider
WHEELBASE	235 cm
TRACK WIDTH	129.6 cm at the front, 131 cm at the rear
WEIGHT (EMPTY)	880 kg

PALMARES

WOLFGANG VON TRIPS
Second, Mille Miglia, Italy, May 11–12, 1957
MIKE HAWTHORN AND LUIGI MUSSO
Second, 1,000 km of Caracas, Venezuela,
November 3, 1957

Champion of the 1957 World Sports Car
Championship

250 TR

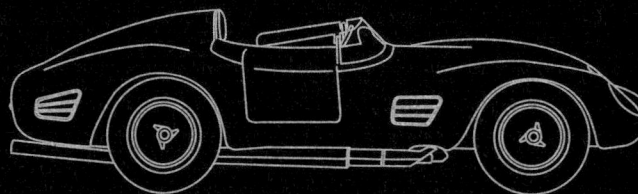

PRODUCTION

YEAR OF PRODUCTION	1958
CHASSIS NUMBER	#0728 TR

ENGINE

TYPE	V12 at 60° (front longitudinal)
ENGINE SIZE	2,953.21 cm^3 (73 × 58.8 mm)
MAXIMUM POWER	300 hp at 7,200 rpm
DISTRIBUTION	1 camshaft, 2 spark plugs per cylinder
FUEL FEED	6 Weber 38 DCN carburetors

CHASSIS

FRAME	Tubular steel
GEARBOX	4 gears and reverse

BODYWORK

DESIGNER	Scaglietti
TYPE	2-seater Spider
WHEELBASE	235 cm
TRACK WIDTH	130.8 cm at the front, 130 cm at the rear
WEIGHT (EMPTY)	800 kg

PALMARES

PHIL HILL AND OLIVIER GENDEBIEN
First, 24 Hours of Le Mans, France,
June 21–22, 1958

Champion of the 1958 World Sports Car
Championship

DINO 246 S

PRODUCTION

YEAR OF PRODUCTION	1960
CHASSIS NUMBER	#0778

ENGINE

TYPE	V6 at 60° (front longitudinal)
ENGINE SIZE	2,417.33 cm³ (85 × 71 mm)
MAXIMUM POWER	250 hp at 7,500 rpm
DISTRIBUTION	1 camshaft, 2 spark plugs per cylinder
FUEL FEED	3 Weber 42 DCN carburetors

CHASSIS

FRAME	Tubular steel
GEARBOX	5 gears and reverse

BODYWORK

DESIGNER	Fantuzzi
TYPE	2-seater Spider
WHEELBASE	216 cm
TRACK WIDTH	124.5 cm at the front, 120.5 cm at the rear
WEIGHT (EMPTY)	640 kg

PALMARES

Champion of the 1960 World Sports Car Championship

330 TRI LM

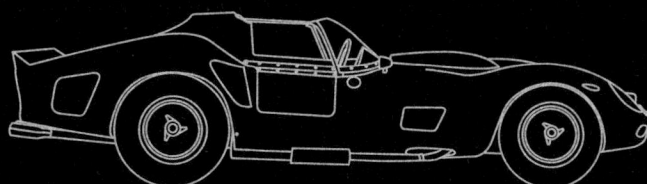

PRODUCTION

YEAR OF PRODUCTION	1962
CHASSIS NUMBER	#0808

ENGINE

TYPE	V12 at 60° (front longitudinal)
ENGINE SIZE	3,967.44 cm³ (77 × 71 mm)
MAXIMUM POWER	390 hp at 7,500 rpm
DISTRIBUTION	1 camshaft, 2 spark plugs per cylinder
FUEL FEED	6 Weber 42 DCN carburetors

CHASSIS

FRAME	Tubular steel
GEARBOX	5 gears and reverse

BODYWORK

DESIGNER	Fantuzzi
TYPE	2-seater Spider
WHEELBASE	242 cm
TRACK WIDTH	124.5 cm at the front, 127.5 cm at the rear
WEIGHT (EMPTY)	820 kg

PALMARES

PHIL HILL AND OLIVIER GENDEBIEN
First, 24 Hours of Le Mans, France,
June 23–24, 1962
PEDRO RODRÍGUEZ
First, 400 km of Bridgehampton, New York, USA,
September 16, 1962
Second, Canadian Grand Prix, Mosport Park,
September 22, 1962
GRAHAM HILL AND PEDRO RODRÍGUEZ
Third, 12 Hours of Sebring, Florida, USA,
March 23, 1963

268 SP

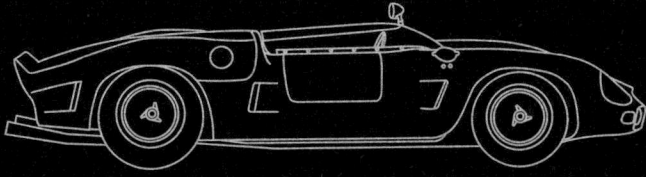

PRODUCTION

YEAR OF PRODUCTION 1962 (248 SP converted into a 268 SP)
CHASSIS NUMBER #0798

ENGINE

TYPE V8 at 90° (rear longitudinal)
ENGINE SIZE 2,644.96 cm³ (77 × 71 mm)
MAXIMUM POWER 265 hp at 7,000 rpm
DISTRIBUTION 1 camshaft, 2 spark plugs per cylinder
FUEL FEED 4 Weber 40 IF2C carburetors

CHASSIS

FRAME Tubular steel
GEARBOX 5 gears and reverse

BODYWORK

DESIGNER Fantuzzi
TYPE 2-seater Spider
WHEELBASE 232 cm
TRACK WIDTH 120 cm at the front, 120 cm at the rear
WEIGHT (EMPTY) 660 kg

PALMARES

Champion of the 1962 World Sports Car
Championship

275 P

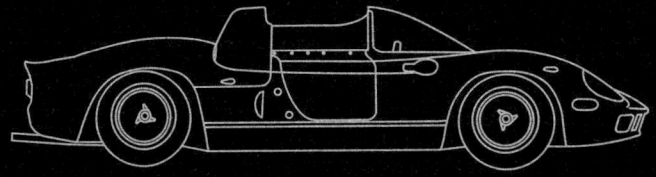

PRODUCTION

YEAR OF PRODUCTION 1963 (250 P, converted into a 275 P in 1964)
CHASSIS NUMBER #0814 (1963), #0816 (1964)

ENGINE

TYPE V12 at 60° (rear longitudinal)
ENGINE SIZE 3,285.72 cm³ (77 × 58.8 mm)
MAXIMUM POWER 320 hp at 7,700 rpm
DISTRIBUTION 1 camshaft, 2 spark plugs per cylinder
FUEL FEED 6 Weber 38 DCN carburetors

CHASSIS

FRAME Tubular steel
GEARBOX 5 gears and reverse

BODYWORK

DESIGNER Fantuzzi
TYPE 2-seater Spider
WHEELBASE 240 cm
TRACK WIDTH 135 cm at the front, 134 cm at the rear
WEIGHT (EMPTY) 755 kg

PALMARES

LORENZO BANDINI AND LUDOVICO SCARFIOTTI
First, 24 Hours of Le Mans, France,
June 15–16, 1963
MIKE PARKES AND UMBERTO MAGLIOLI
First, 12 Hours of Sebring, Florida, USA,
March 21, 1964
JEAN GUICHET AND NINO VACCARELLA
First, 24 Hours of Le Mans, France,
June 21–22, 1964

Champion of the 1963 World Sports Car
Championship

330 P

PRODUCTION

YEAR OF PRODUCTION	1964
CHASSIS NUMBER	#0822

ENGINE

TYPE	V12 at 60° (rear longitudinal)
ENGINE SIZE	3,967.44 cm³ (77 × 71 mm)
MAXIMUM POWER	370 hp at 7,200 rpm
DISTRIBUTION	1 camshaft, 2 spark plugs per cylinder
FUEL FEED	6 Weber 38 DCN carburetors

CHASSIS

FRAME	Tubular steel
GEARBOX	5 gears and reverse

BODYWORK

DESIGNER	Fantuzzi
TYPE	2-seater Berlinetta
WHEELBASE	240 cm
TRACK WIDTH	135 cm at the front, 134 cm at the rear
WEIGHT (EMPTY)	785 kg

PALMARES

JOHN SURTEES AND LORENZO BANDINI
Third, 12 Hours of Sebring, Florida, USA,
March 21, 1964
Third, 24 Hours of Le Mans, France,
June 21–22, 1964

250 GTO

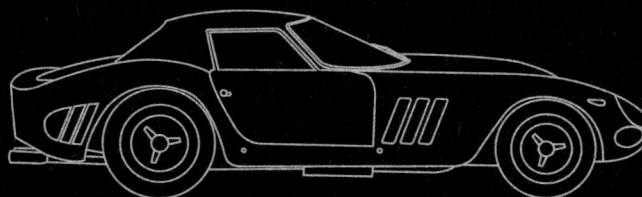

PRODUCTION

YEAR OF PRODUCTION	1964
CHASSIS NUMBER	#5573

ENGINE

TYPE	V12 at 60° (front longitudinal)
ENGINE SIZE	2,953.21 cm³ (73 × 58.8 mm)
MAXIMUM POWER	300 hp at 7,400 rpm
DISTRIBUTION	1 camshaft, 2 spark plugs per cylinder
FUEL FEED	6 Weber 38 DCN carburetors

CHASSIS

FRAME	Tubular steel
GEARBOX	5 gears and reverse

BODYWORK

DESIGNER	Pininfarina, remodeled by Scaglietti
TYPE	2-seater Berlinetta
WHEELBASE	240 cm
TRACK WIDTH	135.4 cm at the front, 135 cm at the rear
WEIGHT (EMPTY)	880 kg

PALMARES

LORENZO BANDINI
Third, 500 km of Spa-Francorchamps, Belgium,
May 17, 1964
JEAN GUICHET AND MIKE PARKES
Second, 1,000 km of Nürburgring, Germany,
May 31, 1964

412 P

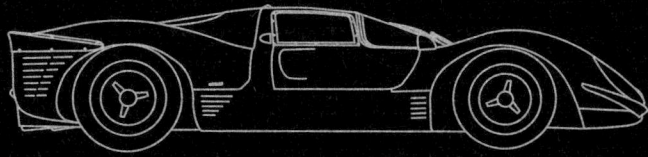

PRODUCTION

YEAR OF PRODUCTION	1966 (330 P3 converted into a 412 P in 1967)
CHASSIS NUMBER	#0844 (1966), #0848 (1967)

ENGINE

TYPE	V12 at 60° (rear longitudinal)
ENGINE SIZE	3,967.44 cm³ (77 × 71 mm)
MAXIMUM POWER	420 hp at 8,000 rpm
DISTRIBUTION	2 camshaft, 2 spark plugs per cylinder
FUEL FEED	6 Weber 40 DCN/15 carburetors

CHASSIS

FRAME	Tubular steel
GEARBOX	5 gears and reverse

BODYWORK

DESIGNER	Drogo
TYPE	2-seater Berlinetta
WHEELBASE	240 cm
TRACK WIDTH	146.6 cm at the front, 148.4 cm at the rear
WEIGHT (EMPTY)	835 kg

330 P4

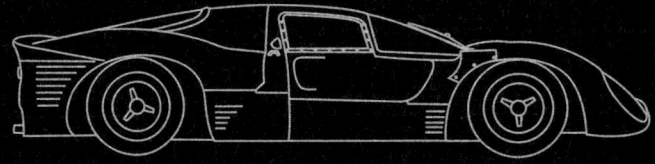

PRODUCTION

YEAR OF PRODUCTION	1967
CHASSIS NUMBER	#0860

ENGINE

TYPE	V12 at 60° (rear longitudinal)
ENGINE SIZE	3,967.44 cm³ (77 × 71 mm)
MAXIMUM POWER	450 hp at 8,000 rpm
DISTRIBUTION	2 camshafts, 3 spark plugs per cylinder
FUEL FEED	Lucas indirect injection

CHASSIS

FRAME	Tubular steel
GEARBOX	5 gears and reverse

BODYWORK

DESIGNER	Drogo
TYPE	2-seater Berlinetta
WHEELBASE	240 cm
TRACK WIDTH	148.8 cm at the front, 145 cm at the rear
WEIGHT (EMPTY)	792 kg

PALMARES

CHRIS AMON AND JACKIE STEWART
Second, BOAC 500, Brands Hatch, Great Britain,
July 30, 1967
CHRIS AMON
Fifth, Can-Am, Monterey, California, USA,
October 10, 1967
Eighth, Can-Am, Riverside, California, USA,
October 29, 1967
Thirteenth, Can-Am, Elkhart Lake, Wisconsin, USA,
September 1, 1967

Champion of the 1967 World Sports Car
Championship

312 P

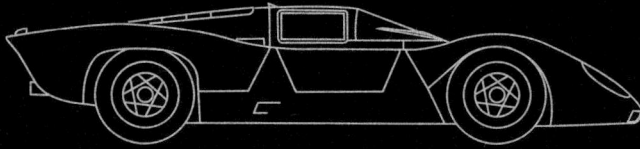

PRODUCTION

YEAR OF PRODUCTION	1969
CHASSIS NUMBER	#0870

ENGINE

TYPE	V12 at 60° (rear longitudinal)
ENGINE SIZE	2,989.56 cm³ (77 × 53.5 mm)
MAXIMUM POWER	420 hp at 9,800 rpm
DISTRIBUTION	2 camshafts, 4 spark plugs per cylinder
FUEL FEED	Lucas indirect injection

CHASSIS

FRAME	Tubular steel with riveted aluminum panels
GEARBOX	5 gears and reverse

BODYWORK

TYPE	2-seater Berlinetta
WHEELBASE	237 cm
TRACK WIDTH	148.5 cm at the front, 150 cm at the rear
WEIGHT (EMPTY)	680 kg

PALMARES

DAVID PIPER AND PEDRO RODRÍGUEZ
Second, 1,000 km of Spa-Francorchamps, Belgium,
May 10, 1969

312 B

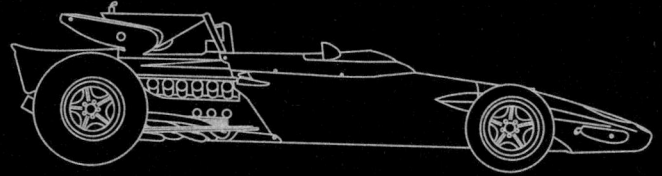

PRODUCTION

YEAR OF PRODUCTION	1969
CHASSIS NUMBER	#001

ENGINE

TYPE	V12 at 180° (rear longitudinal)
ENGINE SIZE	2,991.01 cm³ (78.5 × 51.5 mm)
MAXIMUM POWER	450 hp at 12,000 rpm
DISTRIBUTION	2 camshafts, 4 spark plugs per cylinder
FUEL FEED	Lucas indirect injection

CHASSIS

FRAME	Semi-monocoque, tubular steel aluminum panels
GEARBOX	5 gears and reverse

BODYWORK

TYPE	1-seater F1
WHEELBASE	238.5 cm
TRACK WIDTH	156.57 cm at the front, 157.54 cm at the rear
WEIGHT (EMPTY)	534 kg

PALMARES

JACKY ICKX
Third, Netherlands Grand Prix, Zandvoort,
June 21, 1970
First, Austrian Grand Prix, Spielberg,
August 16, 1970
First, Canadian Grand Prix, Mont-Tremblant,
September 20, 1970
Fourth, American Grand Prix, Watkins Glen,
New York, October 4, 1970
First, Mexican Grand Prix, Mexico City,
October 25, 1970

512 M

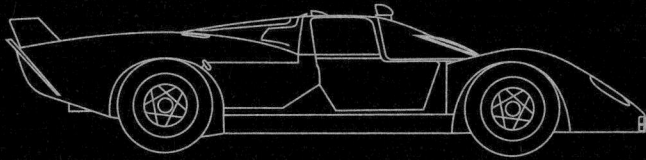

PRODUCTION

YEAR OF PRODUCTION	1970
CHASSIS NUMBER	#1018

ENGINE

TYPE	V12 at 60° (rear longitudinal)
ENGINE SIZE	4,993.53 cm³ (87 × 70 mm)
MAXIMUM POWER	550 hp at 8,500 rpm
DISTRIBUTION	2 camshafts, 4 spark plugs per cylinder
FUEL FEED	Lucas indirect injection

CHASSIS

FRAME	Tubular steel with riveted aluminum panels
GEARBOX	5 gears and reverse

BODYWORK

TYPE	2-seater Berlinetta
WHEELBASE	240 cm
TRACK WIDTH	151.8 cm at the front, 151.1 cm at the rear
WEIGHT (EMPTY)	840 kg

312 P

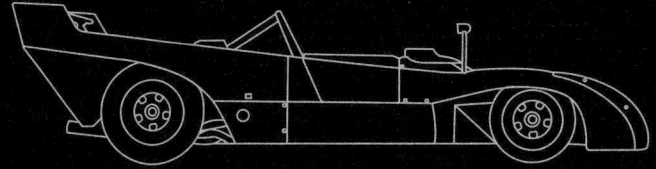

PRODUCTION

YEAR OF PRODUCTION	1971
CHASSIS NUMBER	#0884

ENGINE

TYPE	V12 at 180° (rear longitudinal)
ENGINE SIZE	2,991.01 cm³ (78.5 × 51.5 mm)
MAXIMUM POWER	450 hp at 10,800 rpm
DISTRIBUTION	2 camshafts, 4 spark plugs per cylinder
FUEL FEED	Lucas indirect injection

CHASSIS

FRAME	Tubular steel with riveted aluminum panels
GEARBOX	5 gears and reverse

BODYWORK

TYPE	2-seater Spider
WHEELBASE	222 cm
TRACK WIDTH	142.5 at the front, 140 cm at the rear
WEIGHT	585 kg (with water and oil)

PALMARES

CLAY REGAZZONI AND BRIAN REDMAN
First, 1,000 km of Buenos Aires, Argentina,
January 9, 1972
ARTURO MERZARIO AND SANDRO MUNARI
First, Targa Florio, Italy, May 21, 1972
Fourth, 1,000 km of Zeltweg, Austria, June 25, 1972

Champion of the 1972 World Sports Car
Championship

375 Plus
José Froilán Gonzalez and Maurice Trintignant (#4) win the 24 Hours of Le Mans (France), June 12–13, 1954

250 TR
Phil Hill and Olivier Gendebien (#14) win the 24 Hours of Le Mans (France), June 21–22, 1958

330 TRI LM
Phil Hill and Olivier Gendebien (#6) win the 24 Hours of Le Mans (France), June 23–24, 1962

275 P
Jean Guichet and Nino Vaccarella (#20) win the 24 Hours of Le Mans (France), June 21–22, 1964

330 P4

Chris Amon and Jackie Stewart (#6) finish second in the BOAC 500, Brands Hatch (Great Britain), July 30, 1967

250 GTO
Jean Guichet and Mike Parkes (#83) finish second in the 1,000 km of Nürburgring (Germany), May 31, 1964

312 P
Arturo Merzario and Sandro Munari (#3) win the Targa Florio (Italy), May 21, 1972

3

THE WORLD
OF RACING

JACK SETTON'S COLLECTION

The third section of *Tribute to Ferrari* was entitled "Le Monde de la course" (The World of Racing) and dedicated to French businessman Jack Setton's collection of Formula 1 cars. Known as a major importer of Japanese electronics to France since 1973, Setton—whose father, Joseph, was a lover of nineteenth-century Pre-Raphaelite painting—quickly built up a collection of both Formula 1 cars (Ferrari, Williams, Renault, and Tyrrell) and sports prototypes (Ferrari, Alfa Romeo, Porsche, Jaguar, Ford, Aston Martin, and Matra) from different periods. Like Pierre Bardinon, Jack Setton also built himself a race track, in 1981, on the grounds of his home, Château Wideville in Crespières, west of Paris. "The original idea was to select cars that had won races," he says, "as those were the ones I wanted to drive." For the exhibition, all seven Formula 1 cars on show (except the 625 F1) had competed in Grands Prix in the 1960s and 1970s. John Surtees was crowned world champion in 1964 driving the 158, while among the 312, the T had been driven to the championship by Niki Lauda in 1975, and the T4 by Jody Scheckter and Gilles Villeneuve in 1979. The collection was eventually sold off by Jack Setton over several decades.

Pages 126–27: Aerial view of the Fiorano circuit, Ferrari test track, Italy, 1972.

Above and following pages: Views of the *Tribute to Ferrari* exhibition, 1987
From left to right, top to bottom:
312 B2 (1971), 312 F1 (1968), 312 T3 (1978), 312 T4 (1979), and 312 T (1975)

312 B2 (1971) and 312 T3 (1978)

312 T4 (1979)

312 T (1975)

312 T4 (1979) and 312 T (1975)

312 B2 (1971), 312 F1 (1968), and 312 T3 (1978)

Drivers' portrait gallery, exhibited in the spaces of the "Bunker"

625 F1

512 F1

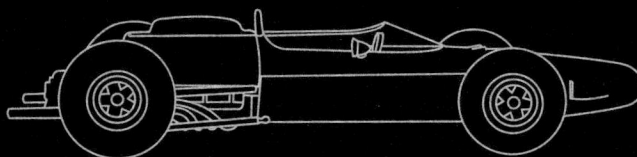

PRODUCTION

YEAR OF PRODUCTION	1955
CHASSIS NUMBER	#0540

ENGINE

TYPE	4 in-line cylinders (front longitudinal)
ENGINE SIZE	2,498.32 cm³ (94 × 90 mm)
MAXIMUM POWER	210 hp at 7,000 rpm
DISTRIBUTION	2 camshafts, 2 spark plugs per cylinder
FUEL FEED	2 Weber 50 DCO carburetors

CHASSIS

FRAME	Tubular steel
GEARBOX	4 gears and reverse

BODYWORK

TYPE	1-seater F1
WHEELBASE	216 cm
TRACK WIDTH	127.8 at the front, 125 cm at the rear
WEIGHT	600 kg (with water and oil)

PALMARES

Alfonso de Portago's personal car

PRODUCTION

YEAR OF PRODUCTION	1964
CHASSIS NUMBER	#0009

ENGINE

TYPE	V12 at 180° (rear longitudinal)
ENGINE SIZE	1,489.63 cm³ (56 × 50.4 mm)
MAXIMUM POWER	220 hp at 12,000 rpm
DISTRIBUTION	2 camshafts, 2 spark plugs per cylinder
FUEL FEED	Lucas indirect injection

CHASSIS

FRAME	Semi-monocoque, tubular steel and aluminum panels
GEARBOX	5 gears and reverse

BODYWORK

TYPE	1-seater F1
WHEELBASE	240 cm
TRACK WIDTH	138 cm at the front, 135 cm at the rear
WEIGHT	490 kg (with water and oil)

158 F1

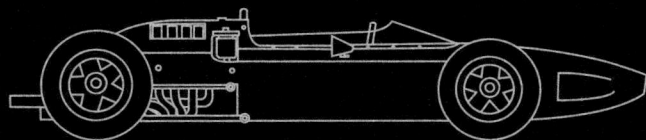

PRODUCTION

YEAR OF PRODUCTION	1964
CHASSIS NUMBER	#006

ENGINE

TYPE	V8 at 90° (rear longitudinal)
ENGINE SIZE	1,489.23 cm³ (67 × 52.8 mm)
MAXIMUM POWER	210 hp at 11,000 rpm
DISTRIBUTION	2 camshafts, 2 spark plugs per cylinder
FUEL FEED	Lucas indirect injection

CHASSIS

FRAME	Semi-monocoque, tubular steel and aluminum panels
GEARBOX	5 gears and reverse

BODYWORK

TYPE	1-seater F1
WHEELBASE	238 cm
TRACK WIDTH	135 cm at the front and rear
WEIGHT (EMPTY)	468 kg

PALMARES

JOHN SURTEES (1964 WORLD CHAMPION)
Second, Netherlands Grand Prix, Zandvoort,
May 24, 1964
Third, British Grand Prix, Brands Hatch,
July 11, 1964
First, Italian Grand Prix, Monza, September 6, 1964
Fourth, Monaco Grand Prix, May 30, 1965

F1 World Constructors' Championship 1964

312 F1

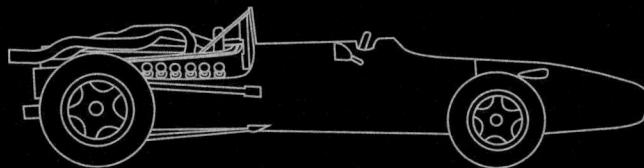

PRODUCTION

YEAR OF PRODUCTION	1968
CHASSIS NUMBER	#0009

ENGINE

TYPE	V12 at 60° (rear longitudinal)
ENGINE SIZE	2,989.56 cm³ (77 × 53.5 mm)
MAXIMUM POWER	410 hp at 10,600 rpm
DISTRIBUTION	2 camshafts, 4 spark plugs per cylinder
FUEL FEED	Lucas indirect injection

CHASSIS

FRAME	Semi-monocoque, tubular steel and aluminum panels
GEARBOX	5 gears and reverse

BODYWORK

TYPE	1-seater F1
WHEELBASE	240 cm
TRACK WIDTH	154.7 cm at the front, 158.2 cm at the rear
WEIGHT	512 kg (with water and oil)

PALMARES

JACKY ICKX
First, French Grand Prix, Rouen, July 7, 1968
Third, British Grand Prix, Brands Hatch, July 20, 1968

TYPE	1-seater F1	TYPE
WHEELBASE	237.8 cm	WHEELBASE
TRACK WIDTH	148.2 cm at the front, 147.5 cm at the rear	TRACK WIDTH
WEIGHT	558 kg (with water and oil)	WEIGHT

PALMARES

PALMARES

CLAY REGAZZONI
First, British Grand Prix, Brands Hatch, March 21,
1971 Third, Netherlands Grand Prix, Zandvoort,
June 20, 1971
Third, German Grand Prix, Nürburgring,
August 1, 1971
JACKY ICKX
First, German Grand Prix, Nürburgring,
August 1, 1972

312 T3

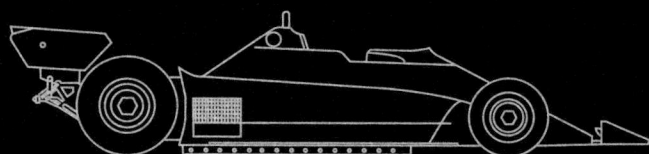

PRODUCTION

YEAR OF PRODUCTION	1978
CHASSIS NUMBER	#032

ENGINE

TYPE	V12 at 180° (rear longitudinal)
ENGINE SIZE	2,991.80 cm^3 (80 × 49.6 mm)
MAXIMUM POWER	510 hp at 12,200 rpm
DISTRIBUTION	2 camshafts, 4 spark plugs per cylinder
FUEL FEED	Lucas indirect injection

CHASSIS

FRAME	Monocoque, light alloy frame and aluminum panels
GEARBOX	Transversal, 5 gears and reverse

BODYWORK

DESIGNER	
TYPE	1-seater F1
WHEELBASE	256 cm
TRACK WIDTH	162 cm at the front, 158.5 cm at the rear
WEIGHT	580 kg (with water and oil)

PALMARES

CARLOS REUTEMANN
First, United States Grand Prix West, Long Beach, California, April 2, 1978

312 T4

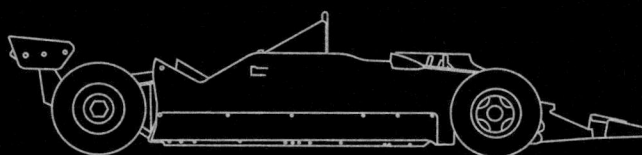

PRODUCTION

YEAR OF PRODUCTION	1979
CHASSIS NUMBER	#039

ENGINE

TYPE	V12 at 180° (rear longitudinal)
ENGINE SIZE	2,991.80 cm^3 (80 × 49.6 mm)
MAXIMUM POWER	515 hp at 12,300 rpm
DISTRIBUTION	2 camshafts, 4 spark plugs per cylinder
FUEL FEED	Lucas indirect injection

CHASSIS

FRAME	Monocoque, light alloy frame and aluminum panels
GEARBOX	Transversal, 5 gears and reverse

BODYWORK

DESIGNER	
TYPE	1-seater F1
WHEELBASE	270 cm
TRACK WIDTH	170 cm at the front, 160 cm at the rear
WEIGHT	590 kg (with water and oil)

PALMARES

F1 World Constructors' Championship 1979

158 F1
John Surtees (#2) wins the Italian Grand Prix in Monza, September 6, 1964

312 B2
Jacky Ickx (#4) wins the German Grand Prix in Nürburg, August 1, 1972

312 B2

Jacky Ickx (#12) wins the Austrian Grand Prix in Zeltweg ahead of Clay Regazzoni (#27), August 16, 1970

312 T
Niki Lauda (#12) wins the French Grand Prix in Le Castellet, July 6, 1975

312 T3
Carlos Reutemann (#11) wins the United States Grand Prix West in Long Beach, California, April 2, 1978

312 T3
Carlos Reutemann (#11) wins the United States Grand Prix West in Long Beach, California, April 2, 1978

312 T4
Gilles Villeneuve (#12) during the Belgian Grand Prix in Zolder, May 13, 1979

4

MECHANICS AND DESIGN

OBJECTS OF DESIRE

Francesca Picchi

Architect, journalist and design historian

1. In 1951, the Museum of Modern Art in New York staged the exhibition *8 Automobiles: An Exhibition Concerned with the Esthetics of Motorcar Design*. In the catalog, Arthur Drexler, future director of the MoMA, commenced his foreword by stating: "Automobiles are hollow, rolling sculpture."

2. Gianni Rogliatti et al., *L'idea Ferrari* (Fabbri Editori, 1990), p. 9. [Unless otherwise specified, all translations are our own and any book titles in Italian are provided purely for context.]

3. When economist John Maynard Keynes analysed what he referred to in his *General Theory of Employment, Interest and Money* as "animal spirits," he included a deeply human factor among economic indicators. It is from this point of view that charisma, vision, passion, as well as idiosyncrasies, perseverance or even just inspired intuition, become factors that are able to influence the success of businesses, and more generally the broader economy. The example of Ferrari thus

Pages 154–55: Technical drawing (diagram and body) of an unrealized car project designed by engineer Alberto Massimino, 1941.

By organizing the *Tribute to Ferrari* exhibition in 1987, the Fondation Cartier pour l'art contemporain created an exhibition that was, in its own way, disruptive. It showed the automobile not only as an object isolated from its context, a "rolling sculpture"[1] with undisputed aesthetic virtues, but above all, for the first time, as the physical expression of an idea evolving over a limited number of years. This fluid form took on many different and distinctive iterations over a range of unique models in an endless quest for perfection.

What connects these models, built at different times, but in such a continuous sequence that they constitute, as a whole, the ultimate representation of the idea of progress? The personality of their creator, Enzo Ferrari. His role is clear in the title of the 1987 exhibition, which today sounds like a celebration held on the eve of his ninetieth birthday, and was probably the most important recognition he received before he died on August 14, 1988. Rarely has the history of a company been so intimately associated with that of its founder. Gianni Agnelli, chairman of Fiat, who became Enzo Ferrari's business partner, said of him: "He managed to transmit his very strong personality to his creations."[2]

Animal spirits: a discontinuity in the history of a region[3]

Enzo Ferrari was a figure who eluded definition. So much so that when he was asked how he would have defined himself, his reply was somewhat unexpected. He said that he felt like an "agitator of men."[4] It is a phrase that he repeated in various forms, sometimes adding a reference to "technical problems," or he would say "agitator of talents, promoter of ideas," but the human element always remained central.

It was a way of alluding to the collective dimension of his company, which was dedicated to fearless experimentation with moving forms. Ferrari's strength was undoubtedly his ability to sniff out talent—first and foremost mechanics and engineers. In fact, Emilia, his native region and the place that shaped him, is an area particularly associated with engineering, to the extent that it is today known as "Motor Valley." From this perspective, there is no doubt that the region plays a leading role in this story and actually helped to create the legend by forming an extended, collective dimension that provided the required background in terms of skills. Those skills were not only linked to the vehicle world (it is notable that Maserati, Lamborghini, Dallara, and Ducati are all based within a few miles), but also to the same concept of engineering as a "mindset."[5]

"Man's imagination is boundless, and nothing precludes him from satisfying this instinct as a splendid, authentic embracer of risk"[6]

It is striking how in Enzo Ferrari's accounts, the car becomes a magical object. In an interview with Italian state television, he said: "The car is something which is part of me, because before seeing it racing on the track it is something I have long dreamed of, have perfected in my mind, and which is the sum of various compromises, sacrifices, and a huge amount of work, both by me and those working with me."[7]

But if he is not exactly a designer, nor an inventor, what exactly is his contribution? "I believe that a constructor, in the broadest sense of the word, has to be the person who has flashes of inspiration, who articulates the formula, nourishes and imagines in his mind the best way to interpret it. The difficult part starts later, when this ideal design has to be assimilated by those who must translate it into a living mechanical being."[8]

Note the use of the word "living": Ferrari often tended to humanize the mechanical. For him, the car was a physical object, but at the same time something that belongs to the realm of human imagination and adventure. The result of pushing rationality beyond its limits, it is also a *fallible* human work, with a powerful dose of irrationality that gravitates around extreme emotions: competition, aggression, speed, the thrill of beating the clock, the love of risk, a passion for research, and teamwork. Ferrari often spoke of the anxiety of being a pioneer[9] and more generally of an adventure marked by a love of extreme conditions. "It is my belief," he said, "that if a designer had to build a car by following the sacred technical automotive texts to the letter, he would end up creating a very honest vehicle, but not a winning one."[10]

His words suggest that a car is the rendering of an evolving idea, not exactly a unique, finished object, but a form in constant evolution: something which moves in space, but also in the dimension of thought. The individual models are very much expressions of a burning passion to the point of accepting the sacrifice of its leading men, the drivers, for whom Ferrari had an "almost mystical"[11] respect. The real protagonist of the scene, the driver, is an entity in and of himself. This is a job for the chosen few who are sufficiently brave and reckless to launch themselves at speeds approaching 300 kmph (200 mph) around the impossible bends of circuits that were built to provide a complete digest of challenges.

becomes emblematic, also in relation to design, because we can say that his personality played a key role in setting in motion virtuous dynamics in an industry that was at the center of the industrial and economic boom following the devastation of the Second World War, creating what remains a highly influential legacy.

4. Enzo Biagi, *Ferrari* (Rizzoli, 1980), pp. 110, 127. "I transformed myself into a designer and manufacturer of engines, into an agitator of talents, a promoter of ideas."

5. The concept of projecting the mind to simulate a phenomenon in order to anticipate the outcome of an action.

6. Enzo Ferrari, *Piloti, che gente...* (Conti Editore, 1985), p. 5.

7. *Correva L'Anno* documentary series, "Enzo Ferrari: l'uomo e la leggenda," with Aldo Piro, Nicola Bertini, Marina Basile, aired October 2, 2015, on RAI Radiotelevisione Italiana.

8. Biagi, *Ferrari*, 128.

9. Biagi, 123.

10. Biagi, 128.

11. Mauro Forghieri and Daniele Buzzonetti, *La Ferrari secondo Forghieri dal 1947 a oggi* (Giorgio Nada Editore, 2012), p. 217.

Fig 1
Fig 2

Fig 1 Enzo Ferrari (background) and Mauro Forghieri (right) during tests of the 330 P2 on the Modena track, 1965.

Fig 2 Designer Gian-Battista Pinin Farina and Enzo Ferrari in the Ferrari factories of Maranello, 1960.

"Evolutionary technical research" is one of the "reasons why we race"[12]

The engineers are some of the most overlooked heroes of this story. Mauro Forghieri was the engineer who worked with Ferrari from 1960 to 1987. He inherited the role from his illustrious predecessors Vittorio Jano, Gioacchino Colombo, and Aurelio Lampredi, but also a whole group that left Ferrari abruptly in 1961, which included Giorgio Chiti and Giotto Bizzarrini. They are just some of the many protagonists of this story which, as already mentioned, has a deeply collective nature.

Forghieri was technical director of the racing stable, and as such at the center of Ferrari mythology from the 1960s onward. He was born in Modena, like Ferrari, whom he described in these terms: "in him, everything was taken to extremes."[13] They spoke to each other in the local dialect with an honesty and directness that was close to brutality at times, cutting through to the heart of the matter and undoubtedly helping to accelerate the decision-making process. Significantly, Forghieri's father, Reclus, had been head of the workshop in the Scuderia's pioneering era, and he was often at his son's side as many bold ideas were put to the test. It is easy to recognize a typical feature of Italian design in this speed of response in the journey from idea to testing, and in the stubborn commitment to experimenting and trying things out. In Italian factories, you are unlikely to hear anyone say: "It can't be done." That would be perceived as an admission of incompetence, a defeatist act, almost cowardice.

Pushing boundaries was a hallmark of Italian design, at least until the 1990s, when a kind of normalization process took hold. Those were more or less the years of the Fondation Cartier exhibition. One cannot overlook the fact that this was the dawn of a technological revolution—1991 was the watershed moment that coincided with the birth of the World Wide Web—and in many ways we can read the exhibition as an intuition of a change that was taking place.

While it tells a unique and extraordinary story, documenting the process of constructing a strong and indisputably recognizable

12. Ferrari, *Piloti, che gente...*, p. 5.
13. Forghieri and Buzzonetti, *La Ferrari secondo Forghieri*, p. 13.

Fig 3

Fig 4

identity, its purpose was to showcase the expressive power of a huge collective effort undertaken outside the logic of established culture. In this expanded and comprehensive appreciation, Ferrari's production output was presented through a range of masterpieces from the collections assembled with painstaking passion by Pierre Bardinon and Jacky Setton.

Constructed around multiple iterations of the object of desire, the exhibition was organized into a series of distinct and spectacular episodes: the road (with the cars parachuted in from above); racing (in the "Bunker"); and the sports prototypes in the amazing carousel of the "History and Legend" section—a sort of evolutionary gallery that adopted the primordial symbols of the circle and the pyramid as its exhibition structure. In the "Village," an exhibition within the exhibition documented the formidable research work conducted over a period of half a century, following the first encounter between Ferrari and Pininfarina (the design company named after its founder, Battista Pinin Farina).[14]

In all this "agitation" of men and ideas, the collaboration with Pininfarina remains the one that more than any other speaks to the artistic. Entirely spontaneously, Farina had developed a sculptor's mindset, leading him to think in terms of being a "modeler of mass and volume."[15] He felt the responsibility of impressing what he defined as "a style based on the most classical canons of beauty" onto a still-evolving form, as the automobile then was. Importantly, in his memoirs he recalls: "I aimed for the lean and essential, I hated all the things that seemed to me like chrome-plated votive offerings applied to vehicles; I learned in my work that taking away was much more effective than adding. We all know well that the superfluous is everywhere."[16]

In the pantheon of talented individuals who were part of Ferrari's adventure, Battista Farina is perhaps the one who was most aware of the artistic dimension of this endeavor. As was Ferrari, in his own way.

Fig 3 Two prototypes Sigma (1969) and Formula 1 ZAZ (1979).

Fig 4 512 S Modulo (1970).

14. Pininfarina was founded in Turin in 1930 as Società Anonima Carrozzeria Pinin Farina. Gian-Battista Farina (known as Pinin, the diminutive of Giuseppe in the Piedmontese dialect, due to his resemblance to his father, whose name it was) founded it when he broke away from Stabilimenti Farina, a kind of bodywork academy established by his brother Giovanni in 1906, where the best talent in the field was trained. In 1961, the brand name was shortened to Pininfarina, merging the family surname and its inventor's nickname.
15. Ernesto Caballo, *Pininfarina, Nato con l'automobile* (Palazzi editore, 1969), p. 208.
16. Sergio Pininfarina, "Prefazione", in *Pininfarina Ferrari: 50 figurini* (Automobilia, 1997), p. 7.

Gianni Agnelli said: "Enzo Ferrari was convinced that an engine was good if it was beautiful; he always said that the most beautiful engine designer would be Palladio."[17]

"The Mille Miglia taught Italians how to make cars."[18]

Every category of objects has its own systems of reference. In the case of Ferraris, the yardstick is racing victories. It would be interesting to trace the evolutionary development of the car through the victories that gradually confirmed the validity of the various mechanical inventions: the engine position; the incorporation of elements to improve the aerodynamics, such as wings (which introduced the concept of using downforce to stabilize the vehicle in corners); progressive weight reduction through experimentation with new materials; the addition of "skirts" to increase the ground effect, and so on.

The epicenter of this "evolutionary technical research," which Ferrari counted among the "reasons why we race,"[19] was the Scuderia's workshop, where he once again demonstrated great mastery by signing up the most inventive individuals. If there is one episode that encapsulates this extraordinary talent for finding the right people, and the creative climate of the postwar years, it is his meeting with Gilberto Colombo, a Milanese engineer and founder of Gilco Autotelai, the "first company specialized in the construction of the tubular chassis." The meeting came about quite by chance. Colombo's family owned a factory making advanced high-precision steel tubes. He went to Modena to negotiate the purchase of a milling machine that Ferrari had managed to make under license from Germany during the war. The two men met and ended up chatting about racing, discovering that they shared the same passion. The meeting went on much longer than anticipated, and Colombo decided to stay for the following day as well. This was long enough to convince Ferrari of the superior dynamic behavior of tubular chassis compared to those made from pressed steel longitudinal members, as used up to that point. The milling machine was not purchased in the end, but an agreement was instead signed that would last a decade, establishing a partnership that had a profound effect on the weight of Ferrari's cars, since as well as being significantly stronger, the tubular chassis proved to be much lighter. Colombo gradually introduced more and more complex and lightweight structures, such as the *tuboscocca* (semi-monocoque tubular chassis), developed specifically for the Ferrari 212, which pre-dated the British spaceframe (skeletal tubular chassis). For the 250 GT—the model which, in 1954, marked the start of an early form of "serial" production of vehicles for an exclusive clientele—Colombo deliberately designed a chassis that would allow efficient assembly.

"Weight is the enemy; wind resistance the obstacle"[20]

The earliest Ferraris—each one unique—embodied a paradox from a design perspective by combining progress in the shape of state-of-the-art technology with the ultimate in traditional craftsmanship. The cars were formed by the expert hands of the panel beaters who shaped the bodywork to cover the frame holding the engine—the heart of the car—like a tailored suit. In the absence of precedents, the practices

17. Biagi, *Ferrari*, p. 128.
18. *La Domenica Sportiva*, "Mille Miglia: Enzo Ferrari," interviewed by Beppe Viola, aired May 16, 1982, on Rai Sport.
19. Ferrari, *Piloti, che gente...*, p. 5.
20. That was the motto of Carrozzeria Touring, the first coachbuilder used by Ferrari. It was founded in early 1926 by two lawyers, Felice Bianchi Anderloni and Gaetano Ponzoni. Around 1935–36, their aerospace-derived Superleggera construction method was revolutionary for the industry. A classic example in Touring's mythology is the Ferrari Le Mans Berlinetta in which Giannino Marzotto won the 1950 Mille Miglia, crossing the finish line wearing a double-breasted coat.

developed by Italy's artisan coachbuilders made use of existing vocabulary, adopting words from the world of fashion such as "dummies" for the cars. But maybe more than the idea of the "tailored suit," it was about being able to "mend" the bodywork, in the sense of stitching or patching. Accidents were fairly frequent, and the availability of knowhow across the region meant that the tools needed—i.e. hands—were readily available to carry out repairs and upgrades to the outer skin. This now lost custom was grafted onto the idea of the car as a changing, mutating object, the result of the assembly of parts, an extraordinary and highly sophisticated jigsaw puzzle of individual pieces that can be disassembled and reassembled in new forms.

An account from Sergio Scaglietti, Ferrari's legendary coachbuilder, may help us to better understand this practice. He was responsible for masterpieces like the 250 GTO and the legendary Testa Rossa—both of which were on display in the exhibition—as well as the 375 MM, built in the mid-1950s for Roberto Rossellini and Ingrid Bergman. His meeting with Ferrari gives an insight into this habit of considering the car as something that can be changed and adapted. Scaglietti, who began working on the shop floor in a bodyshop at the age of thirteen, recounted: "Enzo Ferrari came into the workshop yard by chance and saw a 12-cylinder Ferrari on which I had repaired the bumpers, completely remodeling them and also recessing the headlights, giving the vehicle those futuristic aerodynamic lines…. Ferrari was intrigued and ended up sending all his racing customers to me when their crashed cars needed to be repaired. Finally, he began commissioning bodywork for new cars from me. This led to the first prototypes—my 33 GTOs, and my 15 Testa Rossas, the most beautiful of them. No two cars were the same. They brought the chassis and the wheels to the bodyshop, and I would stretch wire around them and beat the panels over them, giving them their shape, like a sculpture."[21]

Far from being an isolated case, Scaglietti was one of the many talents hidden in that "land that was most adapted to inventive solutions"[22] which Pininfarina talked about on his return from his first trip to the United States, when he had decided to go back to Italy precisely due to the "environmental conditions" he was used to working in. He had discovered that this creative background was lacking on the other side of the Atlantic. It is a concept he mentioned again when describing the role of the Turin environment he grew up in and which reinforced his vocation, working with his brother, who dedicated himself to automobiles after cutting his teeth in coachbuilding for horse-drawn carriages. He had lived through a transitional era and been involved in the transfer of techniques and knowledge between different fields and disciplines. It was a tangible heritage that was difficult to renounce.

Italian bodywork was such vibrant terrain that it gave rise to the phenomenon known in the 1950s as the "Italian line," reflecting the unusual mastery of expression by its exponents. In an entirely instinctive manner, its protagonists lived and breathed a culture strongly influenced by art in terms of its formal models, and by craftsmanship with regard to its practices.

Alfredo Vignale was one of the first coachbuilders to work with Ferrari, before the latter teamed up with Pininfarina. The first vehicle

21. Mara Amorevoli, "Un premio a Scaglietti carrozziere che plasmò la Ferrari," *La Repubblica*, November 26, 2004.
22. Caballo, *Pininfarina, Nato con l'automobile*, p. 119.

Fig 5

Fig 6

Fig 5 Exhaust manifold.

Fig 6 V6 turbo engine.

created for Ferrari in Vignale's bodyshop was a 166 MM coupé built in 1950. At the same time, a collaboration was initiated with Giovanni Michelotti, who over the following years penned a large number of models that have become part of automotive history. Vignale had invented a completely original method for modelling the bodywork: no one else had come up with it, and no one else knew how to use it. His starting point were not full-scale wooden models, or "styling bucks," as used in the premises of Giovanni Farina, which was more or less the academy of Italian bodywork. Rather, Vignale transferred the 1:1 scale drawings onto aluminum sheet metal, with the drawings sometimes being chalked on the floor by Michelotti. The flat sheet of aluminum was first roughly shaped with a wooden mallet on a block, then smoothed with a flat hammer on a sandbag. The final touch was given using a flat hammer on an anvil. Only when it was fixed to the metal structure and finished was the bodywork carefully smoothed out. The sculptural matrix of this process is clear. It was described as a technique similar to the creation of armor in the Middle Ages, but while that may be a rather romanticized notion, it is clear that the artisanal tradition existing in Italy played a key role in enabling this invention.

The largely self-taught creators of this process were, unknowingly, designers. As Aldo Brovarone, the creator of unforgettable models such as the Dino 246, admitted, "in the beginning they called us *figurinisti*, the name used for people who draw fashion sketches, then we became stylists, and now we have become designers."[23] As part of this experimental trial-and-error method, a field of spontaneous research emerged—a prolific territory from a creative viewpoint, with a huge number of people making a contribution to this practice. This was the context in which Ferrari developed its activities.

"These days, you rarely meet anyone seeking to challenge automobile civilization."[24]
Oddly enough, unlike other fields, the car had long held a marginal position with respect to a certain conception of culture and creation.

23. "Copertine d'autore. I grandi designer" Aldo Brovarone, in: *Ruoteclassiche*, thirtieth anniversary edition. Interview by Gilberto Milano, October 14, 2020.
24. Ferrari, *Piloti, che gente...*, p. 5.

Fig 7

Fig 8

Unlike houses, for example, which were the subject of extraordinarily broad cultural investment—at least in Italy, where design, furnishing, and architecture have always been intertwined.

While there are illustrious precedents for the automobile entering a museum of art—the Cisitalia was the first car to become part of the permanent collection of the MoMA—in most cases, the process of presenting cars as museum pieces struggled to move beyond celebrating the aesthetic qualities of the automobile, presented either as the idolization of implicit technological supremacy or as the purest expression of form meets function. It was not until 1951 that the MoMA turned the spotlight on the motorcar as a "rolling sculpture" with an exhibition entitled *8 Automobiles: An Exhibition Concerned with the Esthetics of Motorcar Design.* More than anything else, however, the exhibition aimed to fill the art world's lacuna with regard to the American people's most valued and useful object.

It is no coincidence that the impetus for creating a car culture came from cities that have always had a love affair with an object so symbolic of freedom and movement: Paris, Los Angeles, and, in the case of Italy (the home of Ferrari), Turin. It was in Turin, in 1978, that Vittorio Gregotti—architect, academic, and the first person to write a history of Italian design—worked on the exhibition *Carrozzeria italiana: cultura e progetto*, curated by Angelo Tito Anselmi. The exhibition was put on in a pavilion in Parco del Valentino, a public park in Turin where Enzo Ferrari won the second Turin Grand Prix in 1947 with a 159 S piloted by Frenchman Raymond Sommer. It was the first "critical" exhibition in Italy on the subject, representing a form of compensation for long ignoring a field that had been so key to the country's material culture and the history of industrial design. Seen as neither purely aesthetic nor purely technical objects, automobiles were finally considered as "rather a testament to a complex blend of creative research, of individuals, of intelligent efforts, and hard work."[25] For Gregotti and the academics engaged in bringing about this belated recognition, it was the

Fig 7 The 375 MM produced with a Pininfarina bodywork (1954) remodeled by Scaglietti for the Italian director Roberto Rossellini, 1956.

Fig 8 Sergio Scaglietti and the engineer Tagliaferri, Modena, 1963.

25. Vittorio Gregotti, "Cultura e progetto," *Domus* 585 (August 1978): p. 33.

chance to denounce the "historiographic uncertainties"[26] from which automotive culture suffered. Despite their undisputed leading role in industrial civilization, there is no denying that cars were confined to a sort of "wilderness"[27] at the margins of the cultural world. Having said that, there had been illustrious precedents. Walter Gropius—founder of the Bauhaus—was involved in the design of the Standard 8 for car manufacturer Adler, Le Corbusier designed the Voiture Maximum, while Buckminster Fuller envisioned the Dymaxion car. These incursions, however, were ultimately considered failures as they had no real impact on the great crucible of inventiveness that automotive development had been since its very beginnings.

The fact that carmaking remained at the margins of industrial product culture was not so much due to an inability to make its mark, but because of a more unforgivable blunder: having overlooked "design" as such. That is what Dante Giacosa—the legendary car designer whose work includes the Fiat 600—claims, putting the emphasis firmly on design, defining it as the "essential prerequisite of every product of human ingenuity."[28] The exhibition was, in a sense, the first act of recognition of a fact: spontaneously, the civilization of the automobile had expressed a culture that had been kept at the margins for too long.

The Turin exhibition can be considered the starting point that triggered a wider reassessment, which would take explicit form in the *Automobile and Culture* exhibition held at the Los Angeles Museum of Contemporary Art in 1984, the year the city hosted the Olympic Games. The link between these events, in a way, was Angelo Tito Anselmi, who contributed to both of them. Pontus Hulten—the founding director of the museum at that time—was an intellectual with a particular interest in analyzing the phenomena of spontaneous culture from a cultural standpoint. He did not hesitate to define the LA exhibition as "the first retrospective of automobile design."[29]

Three years later, the Fondation Cartier held an exhibition entirely devoted to the work of Enzo Ferrari. It was the first time that an institution dedicated to art had accorded this level of attention to a phenomenon familiar to everyone, but which had not experienced any deeper appreciation. At the dawn of an era marked by the passage from the "solid" to the "liquid" phase of modernity (according to philosopher Zygmunt Bauman[30]), and precisely because the concept of identity was about to undergo a crisis, Ferrari appeared incomparably solid. It was an exemplary story, which had the advantage of being easily delineated, and thus observable, due to possessing in a sense the Aristotelian unities of time, place, and action. It had a solidity that others did not possess. But above all else, the story recounted the extraordinary enterprise of constructing an undisputed and enduring identity that has remained a dominant global brand right through to the present day. Anselmi wrote that if the automobile had remained a form of "unofficial culture," this was because "it had not been able to recognize itself through the bibliographical, historiographic means which other cultures use with ease."[31] The intellectual investment by highly prestigious cultural institutions therefore appears to be the desire to fill a vacuum in order to facilitate freer movement between the spheres of art, design, and all the spontaneous cultural phenomena that arise from a society's material culture.

26. Vittorio Gregotti, "Introduzione," in *Carrozzeria Italiana. Cultura e progetto*, ed. Angelo Tito Anselmi (Alfieri edizioni d'arte, 1978), p. 7.

27. Angelo Tito Anselmi, "Le grandi esposizioni. Automobiles and culture," *Domus* 655 (1984): p. 88. In his article published on the occasion of the Los Angeles exhibition, Anselmi claims that the "taboo which considered the motor car a savage product with respect to the rules of good design" had finally fallen.

28. Dante Giacosa, "Introduzione," in Giancarlo Busiri Vici, *Atti del convegno Carrozzeria Italiana cultura e progetto* (Marmorata, 1981): p. 7.

29. Pontus Hulten, "Forewords," in *Automobile and Culture*, exh. cat., ed. Gerald Silk (Los Angeles Museum of Contemporary Art, 1985), n.p.

30. See Zygmunt Bauman, *Liquid Modernity* (Polity Press, 2000).

31. Anselmi, *Atti del convegno*, p. 13.

Fig 9

Fig 10

The Paris exhibition chose to entrust the ceremonies around this "liberalization" to the sophisticated designer Andrée Putman, a noted style authority, giving her the opportunity to find a brilliant and playful style with which to welcome and compare these "wondrous objects" as their entrée to the artistic circuit. Irreverent and free, while Andrée Putman was very much at the cutting edge of the intersection between the arts, fashion, design, and decoration, she admitted to a lack of affinity for the world of the automobile, and for the color red, which is so firmly associated with the Ferrari brand. For a designer who stated that she had always suffered a form of "shyness" towards color, we can imagine how intriguing it was for her to be invited to work with a color that she had previously only dealt with in homoeopathic quantities.

The strength of her staging lay in the way she embraced dreamlike fantasy, turning to the world of her childhood to evoke the spirit of the Montgolfier brothers—her ancestors, who invented the hot-air balloon and the parachute. Putman recounted that she had spent all her summers in the Abbey of Fontenay (Burgundy) where the two brothers created their flying machines. She thus benefited from the indelible memory of an adventure inspired by faith in human genius when engaging with science and technology.

From this perspective, the magic circle of red cars grouped together was almost a huge mandala, with the parachutes and hot-air balloons seeming to catch the cars as they descended from the sky. These are signs of an exceptionality, which, while widely celebrated, had been confined to an industry disinclined to emphasize values that were not related to performance and technological prowess. The link to the sky—the domain of dreams and ideas—essentially served to transform the apparatus of the exhibition into a sort of poetic convention in order to lead the gaze beyond the conventional. It was an invitation to the audience to experience the enchanting power of objects that are able to release some of the imagination which produced them (a power even more evident now that their original function is no longer extant). The

Fig 9 and 10 P6 (1969), *mascheroni* (wooden chassis) and preparatory drawings, 1969.

magic circle of sports cars, like the reference to hot-air balloons and parachutes, seems ultimately to have been a means of achieving a more ambitious objective: the creation of a device capable of evoking the same enthusiasm that was sparked in the public by the Montgolfier brothers' undertakings. An indelible memory. A way to reawaken the desire to let oneself be charmed by situations where the boundary between reason and madness becomes less palpable, according to Andrée Putman's idea of style. MILAN, 2025

5

PHOTOGRAPHIC COMMISSIONS

THE IMAGE OF A MODERN LEGEND

We studied books, consulted documents, visited factories and museums, listened to the greatest specialists, and our historical and scientific knowledge became more precise, yet Ferrari's power to fascinate remained total. There was also the problem of how to present it. In these conditions of incredulity, faced with our own powerlessness, we chose to give eleven photographers the mission of bringing us back the image of a modern legend. We explained to them all the names of Modena, Maranello, Imola, Cambiano and, with Christian Caujolle, allocated the subjects based on possible affinities. We had to start completely from scratch. The trouble began when we had the crazy idea of asking Alain Bizos to photograph Juan Manuel Fangio. After several weeks of enquiry that led us from Buenos Aires to Milan, passing through London and Lausanne, we finally had a meeting set up in Brazil. We had enough time for two or three photographs, then off to London, since the rest of the reportage was scheduled for Argentina. Agnès Bonnot took the train to Mulhouse, twice. Franco Fontana, who lived next door, went to Maranello every day. Jeanloup Sieff kindly organized his trip with the Commendatore, and broke his foot after Sergio Pininfarina left him. Pierre-Olivier Deschamps flew off to Italy, but alas, the shoot took place the day after a race in which the red cars didn't win. In Modena, Frank Horvat offered a Testarossa to the locals. And so on: Xavier Lambours, Pascal Dolémieux, François Le Diascorn, Erica Lennard. Maybe Guy Bourdin one day. All made the trip. In their own way. For Ferrari.

Pages 170–71 : Franco Fontana, Ferrari factory, Maranello, 1987.

TEXT PUBLISHED IN THE 1987 EXHIBITION GUIDE

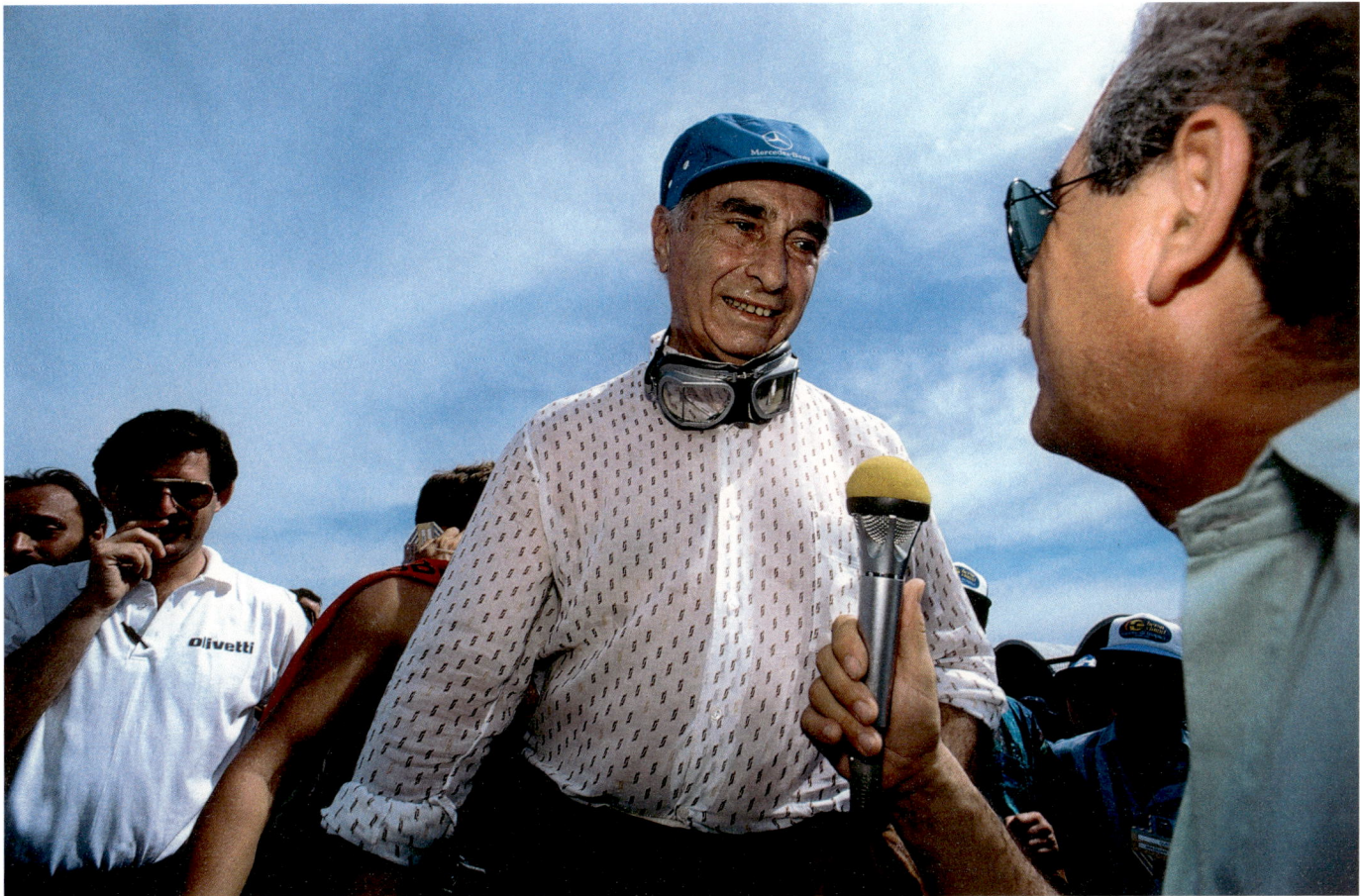

ALAIN BIZOS

Juan Manuel Fangio, Brazilian Grand Prix in Rio de Janeiro, 1987

Michele Alboreto, Brazilian Grand Prix in Rio de Janeiro, 1987

Gerhard Berger, Brazilian Grand Prix in Rio de Janeiro, 1987

AGNÈS BONNOT   Musée national de l'automobile, Mulhouse, 1987

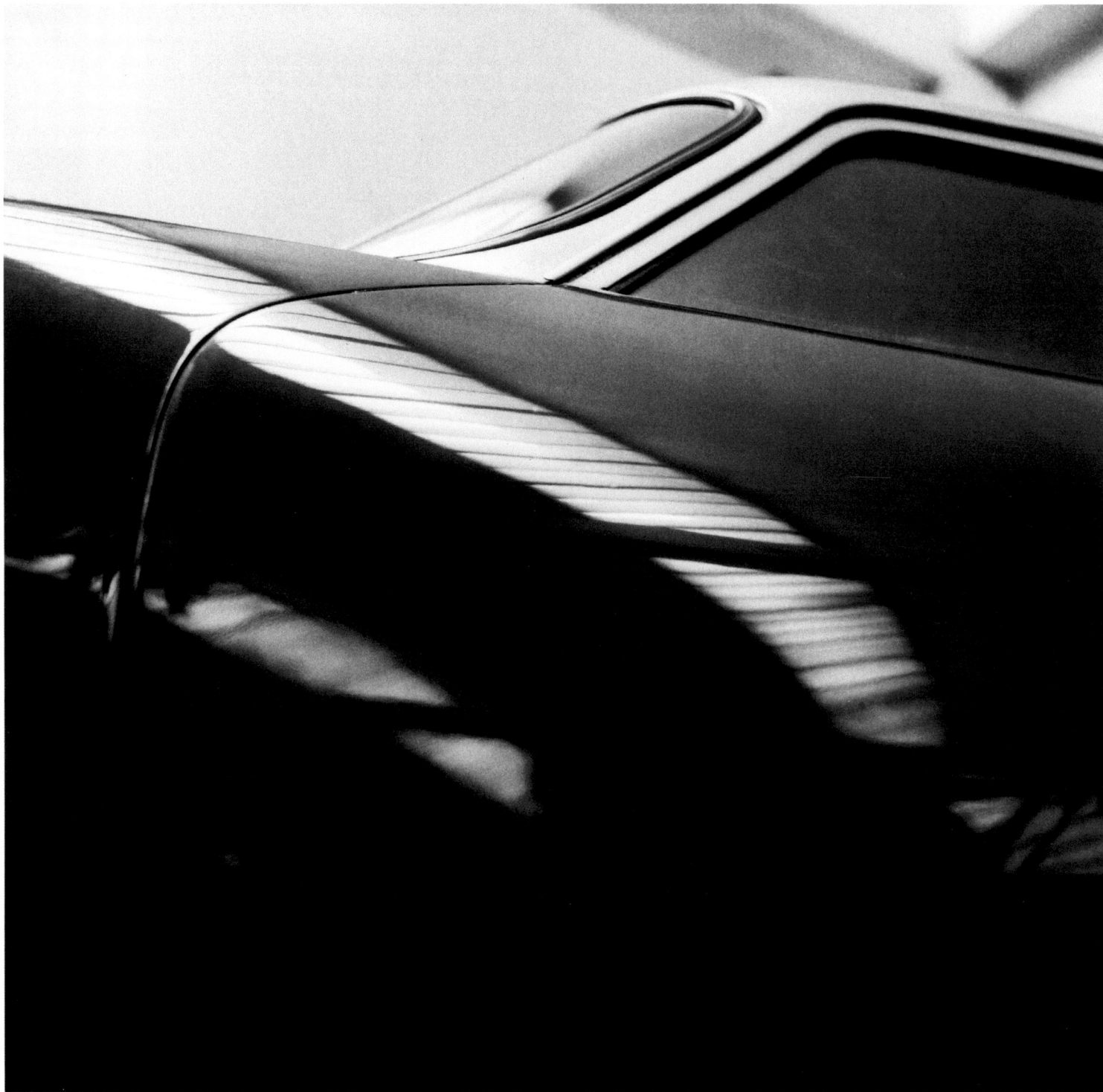

Musée national de l'automobile, Mulhouse, 1987

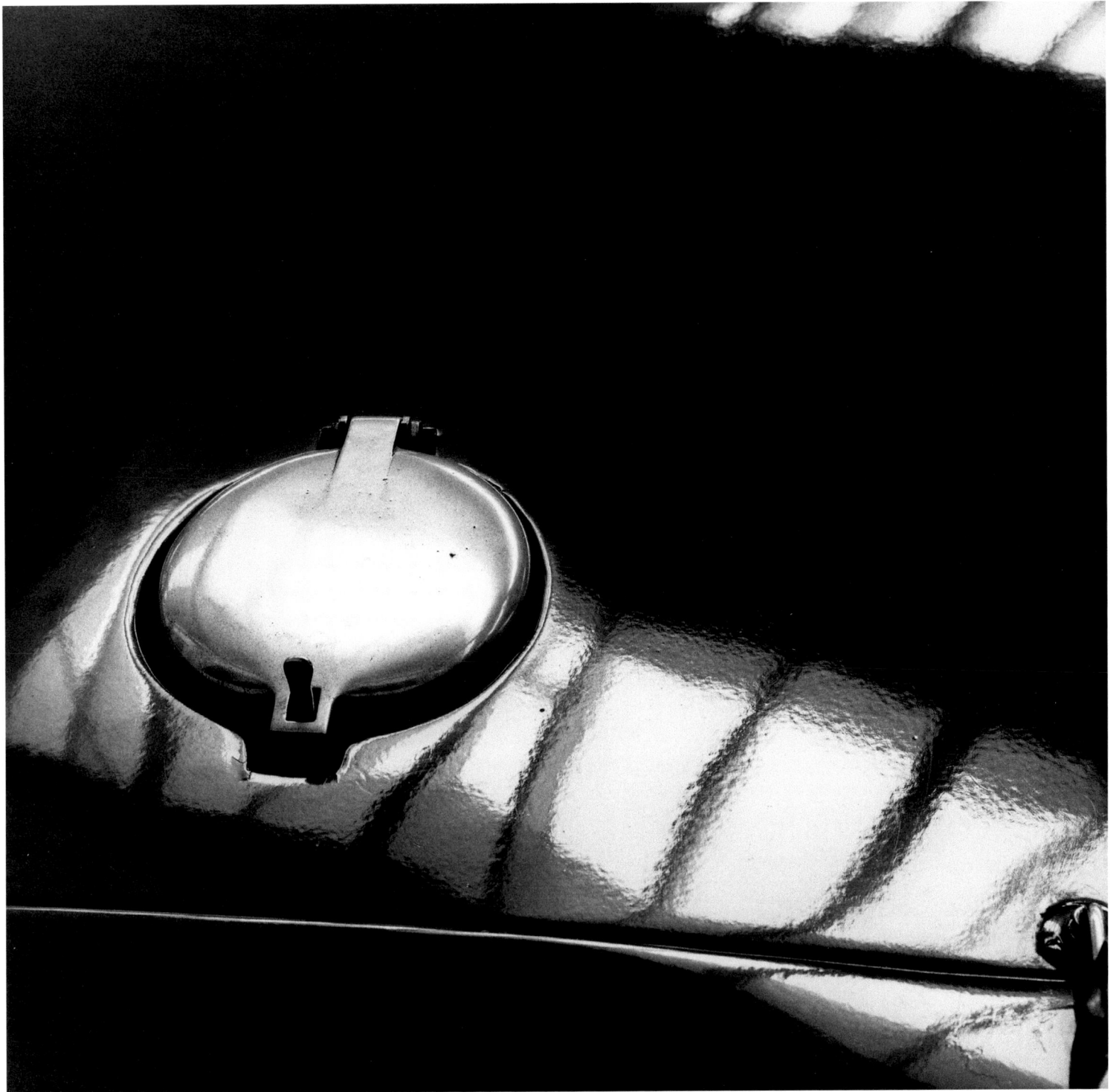

Musée national de l'automobile, Mulhouse, 1987

Pozzi France, Levallois-Perret, 1987

Pozzi France, Levallois-Perret, 1987

PIERRE-OLIVIER DESCHAMPS   Pininfarina factory, Turin, 1987

Ferrari factory, Maranello, 1987

Pininfarina factory, Turin, 1987

Ferrari factory, Maranello, 1987

Pininfarina factory, Turin, 1987

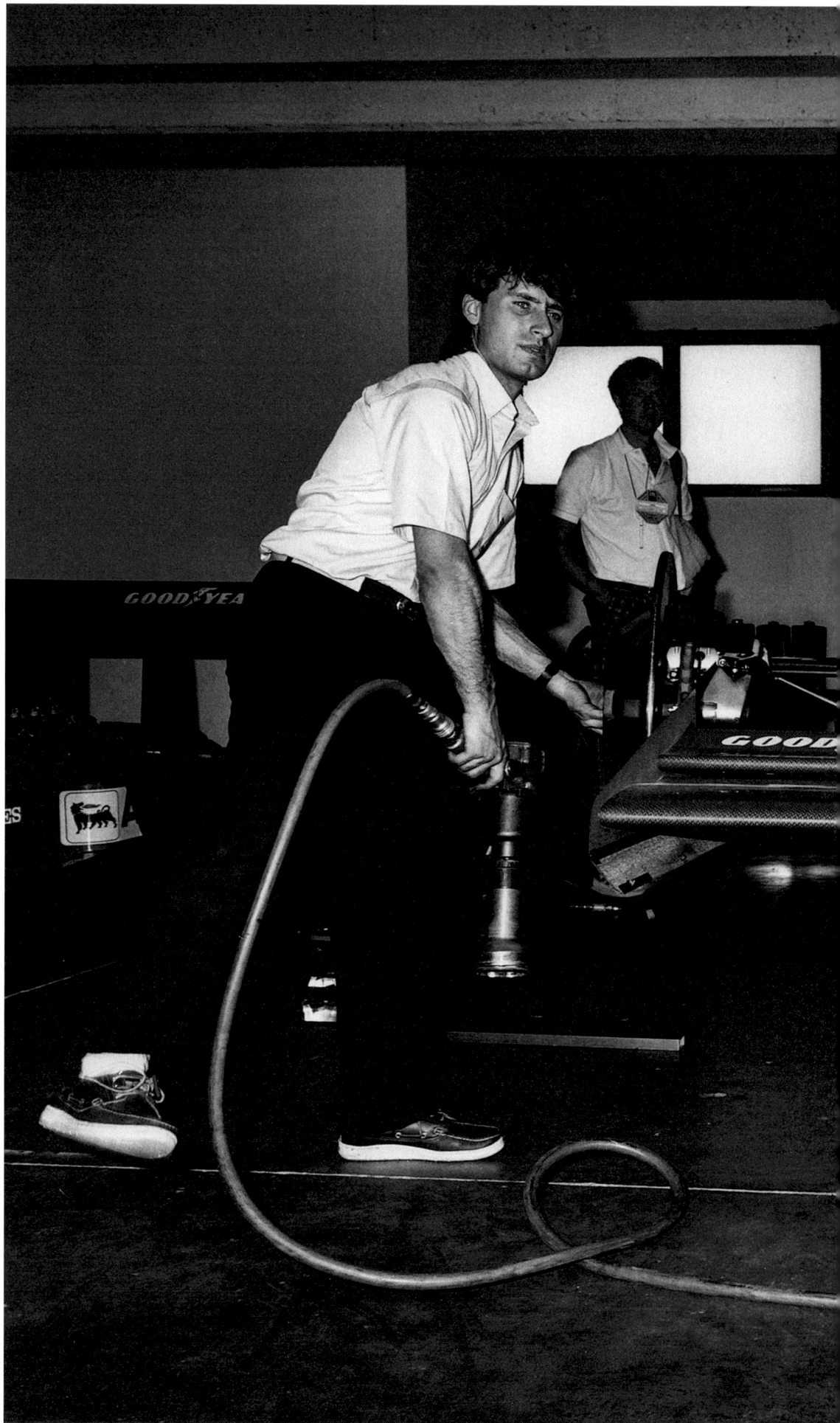

PASCAL DOLÉMIEUX San Marino Grand Prix in Imola, 1987

San Marino Grand Prix in Imola, 1987

San Marino Grand Prix in Imola, 1987

Ferrari factory, Maranello, 1987

Ferrari factory, Maranello, 1987

FRANCO FONTANA   Ferrari factory, Maranello, 1987

San Marino Grand Prix in Imola, 1987

San Marino Grand Prix in Imola, 1987

FRANK HORVAT   Ferrari Testarossa, Modena, 1987

Ferrari Testarossa, Modena, 1987

XAVIER LAMBOURS

Michele Alboreto, 1987

Gerhard Berger, 1987

Piero Ferrari, Maranello, 1987

FRANÇOIS LE DIASCORN   Jack Setton's Collection, 1987

Jack Setton's Collection, 1987

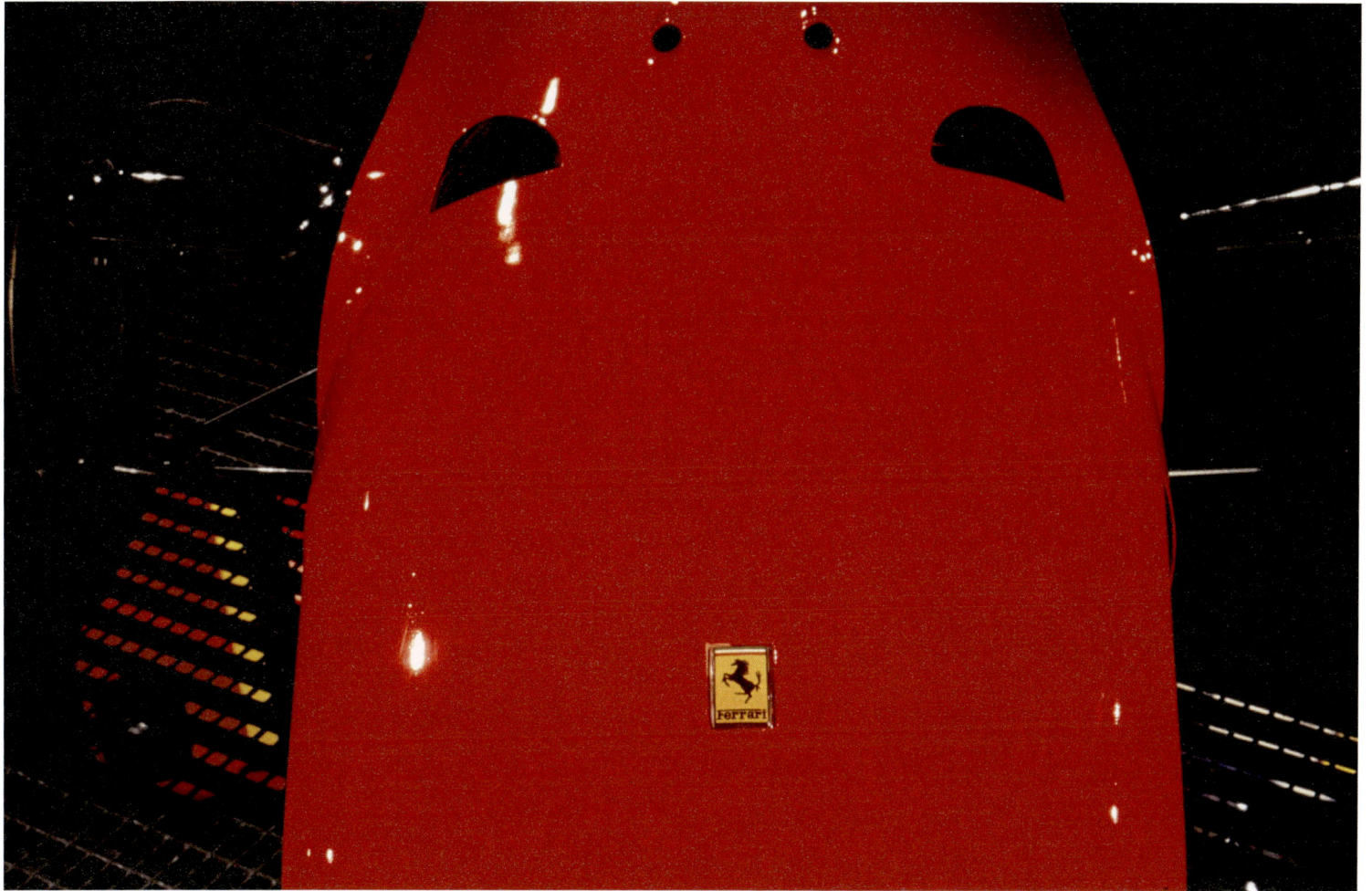

Jack Setton's Collection, 1987

ERICA LENNARD

Mas du Clos, 1987

Mas du Clos, 1987

Mas du Clos, 1987

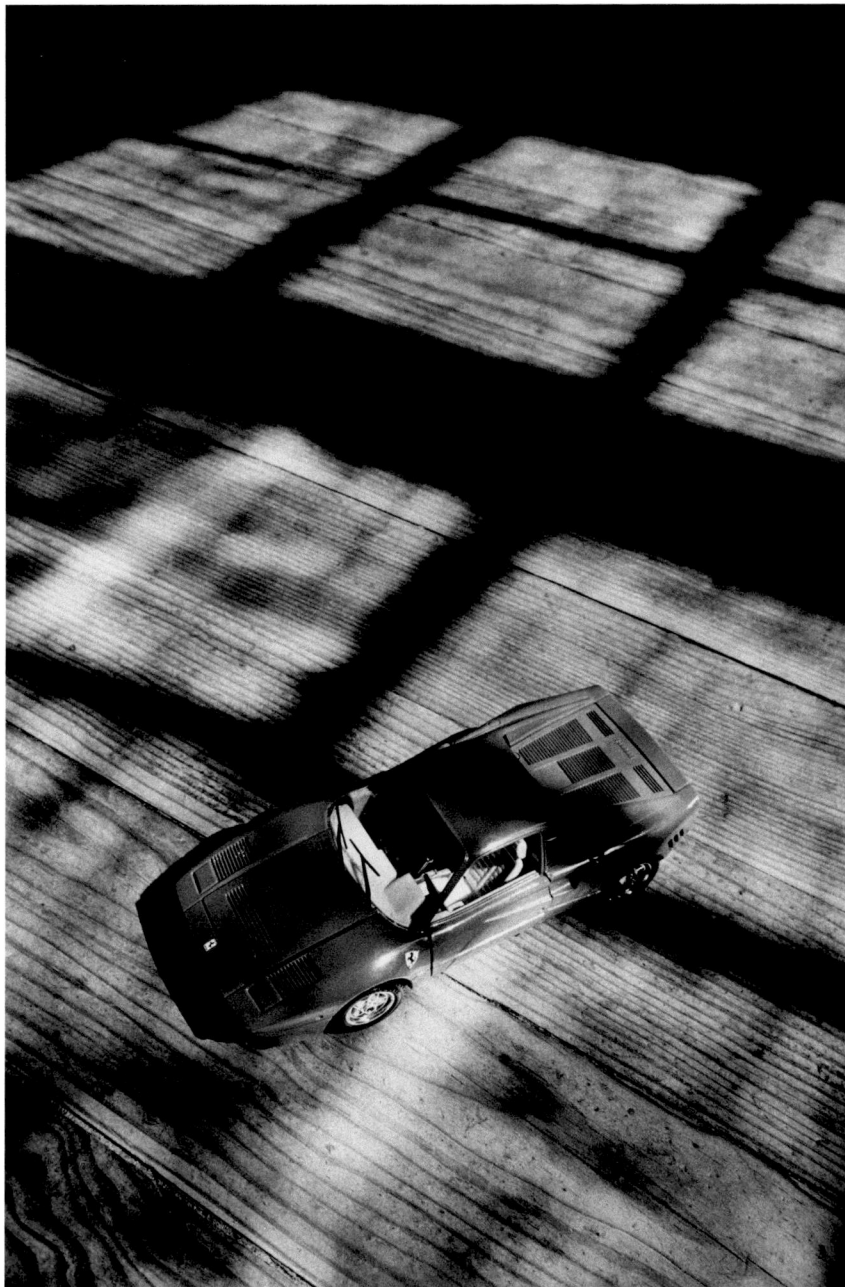

JEANLOUP SIEFF Tribute to Ferrari, 1987

Tribute to Ferrari, 1987

Tribute to Ferrari, 1987

"DON'T WORRY, EVEN AFTER I'M GONE, FERRARI WILL CONTINUE TO EXIST." ENZO FERRARI

Fig 1

Fig 1

Fig 1 Jean Todt in his Maranello office, 2002.

CONVERSATION WITH JEAN TODT
"WHAT I EXPERIENCED IN ITALY WAS UNIQUE"

Philippe Séclier

1. Alain Dominique Perrin (b. 1942) and Jean Todt (b. 1946) both studied at the École des cadres (EDC) in Neuilly-sur-Seine, near Paris, in the 1960s.

2. Hervé Poulain (b. 1940) took part in the 24 Hours of Le Mans in 1975 in a BMW 3.0 CSL decorated by American sculptor and painter Alexander Calder—the first BMW Art Car. It was followed by a car designed by Frank Stella in 1976, Roy Lichtenstein in 1977, and Andy Warhol in 1979.

3. The exhibition, *Les Championnes de César*, was shown at the Fondation Cartier from October 9, 1986 to January 5, 1987.

4. César suggested the creation of a foundation dedicated to artists to Alain Dominique Perrin, then director of Cartier International. The Fondation Cartier pour l'art contemporain opened in Jouy-en-Josas on October 20, 1984.

5. Jean-Pierre Beltoise (1937–2015) was French F3 champion in 1965; European F2 champion in 1968; drove in 88 F1 Grands Prix from 1966 to 1974; and won the Monaco Grand Prix in 1972 in a wheel of a BRM P160B. He also drove in sports-prototype races for Matra.

Alain Dominique Perrin and Jean Todt[1] were brought together by a shared passion for cars and the complicity of two personalities from the world of art, auctioneer Hervé Poulain and sculptor César. In 1985, Poulain—who was a keen motorsport enthusiast alongside his main profession, which he had been practicing since 1969[2]—introduced César to Jean Todt, whom he had first met in 1973 at the Bandama Rally in Côte d'Ivoire. Together, the sculptor and the auctioneer decided to "save" the crashed, wrecked, and written-off 205 Turbo 16s from the World Rally Championship. César made twenty-four of his celebrated "compressions" from four race cars in the workshops of Peugeot Talbot Sport, the team Jean Todt had been managing since 1981. He reduced them to thirty-centimeter-thick plates, then transformed them into artworks—the now-famous *Championnes de César*—that he showed a few months later in 1986 at the Fondation Cartier, at the Domaine du Montcel in Jouy-en Josas.[3]

Alain Dominique Perrin, his friend César, and Jean Todt were reunited soon afterwards in 1987 for the exhibition *Tribute to Ferrari*.[4] Perrin chose Marie-Claude Beaud as artistic director, while Poulain and Todt played essential roles in putting the Fondation Cartier in touch with collectors Pierre Bardinon and Jack Setton, as well as Ferrari's French importer, Daniel Marin, the CEO of Charles Pozzi. Jean Todt was first introduced to Pierre Bardinon in his early twenties by Jean-Pierre Beltoise, who was one of the best co-drivers in rallying and who would become the treasurer of the Mas du Clos Association.[5] Jean Todt remembers being invited to Jack Setton's office in Courbevoie in 1985, where a Ferrari F1 took pride of

Fig 2

Fig 3

place. Setton would become head of Pioneer France and the main sponsor of the Peugeot 205s in rally-raid racing, with their well-known success in the 1987 Paris–Dakar, the same year as *Tribute to Ferrari*. The day of the exhibition's opening—May 22, 1987—Pierre Bardinon, Jack Setton, Jean Todt, and Hervé Poulain were present alongside Alain Dominique Perrin, Marie-Claude Beaud, and Enzo Ferrari's second son, Piero. Six years later, on July 1, 1993, Jean Todt began an extraordinary adventure when he was named general manager of the Scuderia Ferrari in Maranello. During his time there he would write some of the most brilliant chapters in the Scuderia's history; here, he remembers the highlights.

Jean Todt, you were born in 1946, the year before Enzo Ferrari founded his own company and entered his first car, the Ferrari 125 S, into a competition. What is your first Ferrari memory?

When you love cars, you can only love Ferrari. Indeed, my first real sports car was a Ferrari California Spider, with the long chassis. I bought it in the early 1970s and had it renovated by Guy Rivillon, who owned a Ferrari 250 GTO and a garage in Paris.[6] I still have a photo of that California in which I'm posing by the hood at the Linas-Montlhéry circuit.

Did you ever meet Enzo Ferrari? If yes, what was the context and what do you remember about it?

Before talking about Enzo Ferrari, I'd first like to mention Jean Guichet.[7] I met him by chance, one day in the Drugstore des Champs-Élysées [in Paris]. I was with my friend Jean-Claude Lefebvre, we had just bought a copy of *L'Équipe* newspaper and, on the newsstand, I had just spotted the cover of *Sport Auto* magazine featuring Jean and a Ferrari LM. He was a really well-known driver as he'd won the 24 Hours of Le Mans in 1964 with Italian driver Nino Vaccarella, at the wheel of a Ferrari 275 P. But I really got to know him in 1968 when we both competed in the Tour of Corsica in an Alpine A 110. Since then, we have remained firm friends. In 1970, Jean offered to introduce me to Enzo Ferrari. So, we drove to

Fig 2 Jean Todt and César during the creation of a compression from a series 205, in 1986. That same year, César exhibited a set of works made from Peugeot Talbot Sport cars in the exhibition *Les Championnes de César* at the Fondation Cartier pour l'art contemporain.

Fig 3 Luca di Montezemolo and Jean Todt at the finish line of the French Grand Prix in Magny-Cours, July 21, 2002.

6. Guy Rivillon (1930–1997) drove in numerous rallies and hill-climbing races.
7. Jean Guichet (b. 1927) drove for the Scuderia Ferrari between 1963 and 1967, winning five races in a sports-prototype car, including the 24 Hours of Le Mans in 1964, as well as the automobile Tour de France in 1963, alongside José Behra (1924–1997) at the wheel of a Ferrari 250 GTO.

Maranello from Paris in his Mercedes 600. I remember that we'd only just arrived in his office—which two decades later would become mine—when Enzo Ferrari asked Jean in Italian who was the young man he was with. "Usually, you're surrounded by pretty girls!" he added. That's the first image I've kept of him.

My second memory tied to Enzo Ferrari was in 1985. Peugeot had just been crowned World Rally Constructors' champion, and we decided to celebrate by publishing a book that would be sold in shops and distributed at Peugeot garages. I was asked to choose someone to write the book's preface; there was really only one person in my eyes: Enzo Ferrari. At the time I was the representative of sporting manufacturers at the Bureau permanent international des constructeurs automobiles (BPICA) and Marco Piccinini, the sporting director of Scuderia Ferrari, was present at one meeting, so I asked him if he could help get me into the good graces of his boss. Which is how a lunch was organized with Enzo Ferrari, his son, Piero, and Franco Gozzi, the director of communications. The five of us got together at Enzo's house in Fiorano, just next to the private test track. Enzo Ferrari wrote an affectionate letter to me just after that first meeting, dated September 11, 1985, which I have kept safe and is reproduced in the book. The fact remains, though, that during all those years I spent running Peugeot Talbot Sport, I could never have imagined what would happen next.

For you, was there one significant event at Scuderia Ferrari that you remember from before you became sporting director in 1993?
I don't have one particular memory, even if I've followed all the races on the international calendar as long as I've been involved in motor sport, so since the mid-1960s. I greatly admired the drivers Jim Clark and Dan Gurney.[8] Two dramatic events involving Ferrari do come to mind, like flashes: endurance driver Ignazio Giunti's lethal accident during the Buenos Aires 1,000 km in 1971, following a collision on the edge of the track with Jean-Pierre Beltoise's Matra, which had run out of fuel; and Didier Pironi's accident at Hockenheim in 1982, during practice for the German Grand Prix in wet conditions, which marked the end of his Formula 1 career.

In 1993, you were running Peugeot Talbot Sport and had a historic one-two-three at the 24 Hours of Le Mans with the 905. You were also preparing to join the Scuderia Ferrari on July 1. When did you first make contact with Maranello?
In July 1992, I got a call from Bernie Ecclestone, who was then chairman of FOM [Formula One Management, which owned Formula 1]. He told me that Ferrari was in a really bad way and that the team needed to become competitive again quickly for the good of the sport. He thought I was the right man to try to turn the Scuderia around.[9] Ecclestone wasn't the first person to talk to me about Ferrari, though. Jack Setton had also slipped my name to his good friend Gianni Agnelli. Bernie Eccleston had also talked to Luca di Montezemolo, president and managing director of Ferrari, as well as Cesare Romiti, president of Fiat, and Agnelli himself. Immediately afterward, he suggested I call Montezemolo, and we met in August 1992 at his home in Bologna, so we didn't arouse the suspicions of the Italian media. The two of us had a long meeting, and a few weeks

8. Dan Gurney drove in four F1 Grands Prix for Ferrari in 1959.
9. At that time, the last drivers' world championship for Ferrari dated back to 1979 with the South African driver Jody Scheckter; the last constructors' championship to 1983. In 1992, a year before Jean Todt's arrival, Ferrari finished only fourth in the constructors' world championship.

later we met again at my home in Paris. I wanted to leave Peugeot and, despite everyone—including Alain Prost, who had just left Ferrari at the end of the 1991 season—telling me that I wouldn't last, in March 1993 I signed my contract with Ferrari to join the Scuderia. My recruitment was made official on May 11, and I left my office on Avenue de la Grande-Armée in Paris on June 30. On Thursday July 1, at around 10 a.m., team manager Sante Ghedini collected me from my home so that I could head, in a Lancia, to the Magny-Cours circuit for the French Grand Prix, wearing my new red outfit.

You were the second foreign manager to head up Scuderia Ferrari, after the Swiss Peter Schetty in 1971–72. How did you feel when you signed your contract? A mix of amazement and pride? A certain amount of pressure, too?

It was definitely a surprise, but neither amazement nor pressure. At least not at the time. That came later. Pride, certainly. Everyone warned me against going. They kept telling me that it couldn't work, that it was mission impossible. But in the end, I went. The Italian media had a really negative view of my arrival in Maranello and even within the Scuderia itself, it was said out loud that I knew nothing about it. A Frenchman from the world of rallying and endurance racing, who on top of everything had never worked in Formula 1—he wasn't going to stick around for long.

What was your very first task when you arrived at Maranello?

First of all, I observed and analyzed, and tried to understand. Montezemolo had openly given me information about the Scuderia's sporting and technical situation during our earlier meetings. I was also able to rely on Claudio Lombardi, who was in charge of engines; Harvey Postlethwaite, who managed the chassis; and John Barnard, head of Ferrari Design Development (FFD) in the UK. So I talked to them, as well as all the engineers, mechanics, and other people involved in the F1 team. At the time, four hundred people were working for Scuderia Ferrari. Even though we won the German Grand Prix with Gerhard Berger in 1994, and the Canadian Grand Prix the following year with Jean Alesi—which turned out to be his only F1 victory—I knew that it was going to be difficult, and above all long, to make Ferrari successful again.

Michael Schumacher was a double world champion in 1994 and 1995 with Benetton. When did you decide to bring him to Ferrari? Were there any other drivers in the running?

To be honest, the first driver I contacted was Ayrton Senna. I met him at the 1993 Italian Grand Prix, and during our discussions, he told me that he wanted to race for Ferrari from 1994. I told him that, unfortunately, it wouldn't be possible; we weren't ready, and I had two drivers under contract, Gerhard Berger and Jean Alesi. Ayrton retorted that in F1, a contract means nothing. I told him gently that, as far as I was concerned, I had to respect them. On the other hand, I confirmed that we were really interested in his joining us for the 1995 season. But he decided to leave McLaren at the end of 1993 and join the Williams team in 1994, with the dramatic consequences we now know.[10] The next most qualified driver who could join the team was obviously Michael Schumacher, the 1994

10. Ayrton Senna died driving a Williams-Renault FW16 on May 1, 1994, at the circuit of Imola, during the San Marino Grand Prix.

Fig 4
Fig 5

Fig 4 Jean Todt and Michael Schumacher on the starting grid of the French Grand Prix (Magny-Cours), July 21, 2002

Fig 5 Technical meeting in the Scuderia Ferrari motorhome after qualifying trials at the Italian Grand Prix in Monza, September 14, 2002.

11. Niki Lauda (1949–2019) was with Ferrari between 1974 and 1977, driving in fifty-seven Grands Prix and winning fifteen times for the Scuderia. He was world champion in 1975 and 1977, and won a third title, for McLaren, in 1984.
12. Adrian Newey (b. 1958) worked for Williams and McLaren before becoming technical director at Red Bull Racing, the team with which he won six constructors' world titles. He was wanted by Scuderia Ferrari for the 2025 season, but opted to join the Aston Martin F1 team.
13. On November 11, 1997, the World Motorsport Council at the FIA delivered its verdict disqualifying Michael Schumacher from the 1997 championship for dangerous driving in the European Grand Prix in Jerez. The German driver nevertheless conserved his wins, points, pole positions, and best laps from the season. No penalty was imposed on Scuderia Ferrari, which came second in the constructors' championship.

world champion, who would win for a second time in a row in 1995. The first contact was made through Niki Lauda, who spoke to his manager, Willi Weber, in spring 1995.[11] I met them both, accompanied by our lawyer Henry Peter, for the first time in early August at the Hôtel de Paris in Monaco. At the end of a really long day, we signed an agreement in principle for a three-year contract.

It's sometimes forgotten, or at least it wasn't widely publicized at the time, but alongside Michael Schumacher's move, you also recruited two other members of the Benetton team: technical director Ross Brawn and engineer Rory Byrne. Was it hard to convince these technicians to come? They already had great reputations in Formula 1.

Michael's arrival at Ferrari for the 1996 season obviously changed things. He knew I was involved in restructuring the team. I had also hired the aerodynamics specialist Gustav Brunner, but above all I was looking for a technical director. My first choice was Adrian Newey, but he didn't want to join us.[12] So I contacted Ross Brawn. Michael, who had worked with him at Benetton, was obviously aware of the situation and really happy with the choice. Finally, I needed a chief designer, and I thought of Rory Byrne, who had also worked for Benetton. I negotiated for many months with them both, without either of them knowing that I wanted the other at Ferrari. In any case, it was really urgent to have reinforcements of this standard because during the spring of 1996, and despite Michael's first victory for Ferrari at the Spanish Grand Prix in Barcelona, the pressure was mounting. I came really close to being fired at that point. In 1997, we won four Grands Prix, thanks to Michael. But he lost the title to Jacques Villeneuve in the last race in Jerez (Spain), when Michael ran into him.[13] In 1998, Michael won six Grands Prix, but it still wasn't enough—Mika Häkkinen won the last Grand Prix in Suzuka, and the title. Michael had taken pole position, but his engine stalled on the grid. Then he suffered a puncture during the race and had to retire. Ferrari did win the constructors' world title in 1999, after a chaotic season marked by Michael's

Fig 6

accident at Silverstone, when he went off the track and suffered a double tibia-fibula fracture. I knew full well that if he didn't win the drivers' championship in 2000, then I would be out. Fortunately, I was able to count on my family and friends. Every Wednesday—and I mean *every* Wednesday—Pierre Bardinon would call me. When I was appointed to run the Scuderia, Pierre was really happy for me, and he remained one of my most loyal supporters right up to the end.

The *tifosi*[14] know what happened next: between 1993 and 2008, the Scuderia won 106 Grands Prix under your management, with 14 world drivers' and constructors' titles.[15] Yet, you almost left Ferrari at the end of the 2005 season...
I never thought anything was inevitable. I was always searching for the tiniest details, which didn't stop us sometimes suffering setbacks. In any case, I decided to leave at the end of 2005, after twelve full seasons. I had promised Max Mosley that if he were to step down as FIA president, I would put myself forward as his successor. So, in a way, I was committed. But when I spoke to Luca di Montezemolo about it, he asked me to stay on. In the meantime, on June 1, 2004, I had been appointed managing director of Ferrari to look after the whole company, at the same time as Montezemolo became president of Fiat and of Confindustria, the

Fig 6 Michael Schumacher and Jean Todt on the podium of the Japanese Grand Prix in Suzuka, October 8, 2000, after the victory of the German driver, who took home the first of his five consecutive global titles with Ferrari.

14. *Tifosi* in Italian means a group of supporters.
15. Michael Schumacher won the F1 drivers' title with Ferrari five times (2000–04); the most recent driver to win the title for the Scuderia was the Finn Kimi Räikkönen in 2007.

Italian industrial association. I spent my mornings managing the sporting side, and my afternoons working on the industrial and commercial sides. I ended up leaving Ferrari in April 2009 and succeeded Mosley in December 2009.[16]

If you had to single out one memory from your time with Ferrari, what would it be?

The podium at the 2000 Japanese Grand Prix in Suzuka, when I hoisted Michael onto my shoulders to celebrate his first World Drivers' Championship title with Ferrari. It was the greatest moment of my career. I remember standing on the stairs leading to the podium and saying to him: "Our lives will never be quite the same again. We got what we wanted." Even though I realize that all of that is completely meaningless when you know how suddenly a life can be turned upside down.[17]

You succeeded in bringing Ferrari back to the top of its game and you left as the most successful Scuderia director in its history. Nevertheless, do you have any regrets about the seventeen years you spent in Maranello?

Yes, of course, I have regrets. Such as having lost the drivers' title for Michael in 1997, 1998, 1999, 2005, and 2006, and in 2008 for Felipe Massa during the final Grand Prix in his home race in Brazil—which on top of everything was the result of Renault cheating at the Singapore Grand Prix.[18] The job was probably the most difficult of my career, as well as the most exhilarating. Life is a journey, a path. A destiny, too. You never know the route you're going to take, and it can be full of pitfalls. But in the end, the one I chose took me to Ferrari—and what I experienced in Italy was unique.

16. Jean Todt was president of the FIA from October 2009 to December 2021. In September 2010, he co-founded, with Professor Gérard Saillant, the Institut du cerveau et la moelle épinière (ICM, Brain and Spinal Cord Institute) at the Hôpital de la Pitié-Salpétrière in Paris (known as the Institut du cerveau since 2020). Michael Schumacher was one of the founding members. Since 2015, Jean Todt has been the United Nations Secretary-General's Special Envoy for Road Safety.
17. Michael Schumacher (b. 1969) was the victim of a serious skiing accident on December 29, 2013, in the French resort of Méribel. Since then, no information about his state has been released by his family or friends.
18. The 2008 Singapore Grand Prix was marked by what became known as "Crashgate" when Nelson Piquet Jr. deliberately crashed on lap 14. It was later proved that Renault's team principal Flavio Briatore and engineer Pat Symonds had planned the accident to help Piquet's teammate, Fernando Alonso, to victory by bringing out the safety car just after his pit stop. Felipe Massa in a Ferrari was leading the race at the time, but eventually finished second, losing precious points in the world championship, which was won that year—at the season's last Grand Prix, held in Sao Paulo—by Lewis Hamilton in a McLaren.

A FERRARI CHRONOLOGY

Jean-Louis Moncet

1947

After having founded the Scuderia Ferrari in 1929, Enzo Ferrari creates Ferrari Automobili, a company dedicated to the design, construction, and commercialization of high-performance racing and endurance cars.

Enzo Ferrari himself tests the 125 S race car, without bodywork, on the road between Maranello and Formigine on March 12, reaching a speed of around 150 kmph (90 mph) and an estimated power output of 90 hp for 6,000 rpm.

On May 11, a Ferrari 125 C driven by Franco Cortese enters its first track race in Piacenza. It shares the front line of the grid with a Maserati 1500 and a BMW 328. Cortese is forced to drop out of the race while leading, but on May 22, he drives his Ferrari to its first track victory during a race in Rome.

1948

On May 1 and 2, Ferrari wins its first victory at the Mille Miglia endurance race with drivers Clemente Biondetti and Giuseppe Navone in a 166 S Berlinetta Allemano.

1949

On June 25 and 26, Ferrari wins its first 24 Hours of Le Mans endurance race with drivers Luigi Chinetti and Lord Selsdon in a 166 MM Barchetta.

1950

The World Drivers' Championship—which would later become the Formula 1 World Championship—begins on May 13 at Silverstone in the United Kingdom. On the same date, however, the Scuderia Ferrari takes part in an F2 Grand Prix in Mons, Belgium, with a 166 F2. Ferrari subsequently races in Formula 1 and Formula 2 in Europe, Argentina, and Brazil.

On May 21 in Monaco, Ferrari takes part in its first World Drivers' Championship Grand Prix, the second race on the calendar after Silverstone; Alberto Ascari finishes second in a Ferrari 125 F1.

1951

On July 14 at Silverstone, Ferrari takes its first victory in the Formula 1 championship, with Argentine driver José Froilán González behind the wheel of a 375, powered by a naturally aspirated, 4.5-liter V12.

On November 25, during the Carrera Panamericana, Ferrari achieves its first one-two finish with Piero Taruffi and Luigi Chinetti and Alberto Ascari and Luigi Villoresi, both duos driving 212 E Vignale Berlinettas.

1953

Alberto Ascari wins his second world title, again driving a 500 F2.

Ferrari launches production of the 250 MM, first unveiled at the 1951 Paris Motor Show. This Berlinetta, famous for its racing version but also as a Gran Turismo (GT), becomes the first in a long line of classics.

1954

José Froilán González and Maurice Trintignant win the 24 Hours of Le Mans, held on June 12 and 13, in a 375 Plus.

1956 Eugenio Castellotti (#14) in a Ferrari D50 during the Italian Grand Prix in Monza.

1957 Presentation of the 250 Testa Rossa at the Ferrari factory.

1961 Phil Hill (#4) on a 156 F1 at the German Grand Prix in Nürburg.

1955

On May 26, Alberto Ascari dies while testing the 750 Monza Sport. His death, along with financial difficulties, persuades Gianni Lancia—for whom Ascari drove in Formula 1—to pass on the Scuderia Lancia, including the highly innovative D50 race car, to Ferrari, whose 625 and Supersqualo were achieving mixed results.

1956

Dino Ferrari, Enzo's eldest son, dies of muscular dystrophy on June 30 at the age of twenty-four.

Juan Manuel Fangio becomes world champion for the fourth time and for the first time driving a Ferrari, the D50.

1957

Ferrari comes in first, second, and third at the Mille Miglia, held on June 11 and 12. During the race, Alfonso de Portago and Edmund Nelson (the Ferrari fourth team) have a fatal accident and plow into around thirty spectators. The race is never held again.

In November, Ferrari launches one of its most celebrated models: the 250 Testa Rossa.

1958

On June 21 and 22, Olivier Gendebien and Phil Hill win the 24 Hours of Le Mans driving a Ferrari 250 TR58.

1960

On May 29, a Ferrari 246 P driven by Richie Ginther races in the Monaco Grand Prix, alongside the Scuderia's Dino 246. It is the first Ferrari single-seater with a rear engine to feature in a Formula 1 Grand Prix. Its first appearance was as part of the non-world championship International Trophy at Silverstone.

On June 25 and 26, Olivier Gendebien and Paul Frère win the 24 Hours of Le Mans in a Ferrari 250 TR 59-60.

1961

On June 10 and 11, Olivier Gendebien and Phil Hill win the 24 Hours of Le Mans in a Ferrari 250 TRI.

On September 10, Phil Hill, driving a rear-engine Ferrari 156, is crowned Formula 1 world champion, and Ferrari wins the constructors' championship—a title created in 1958—for the first time.

Enzo Ferrari fires Carlo Chiti and his entire technical team, after the engineer disagrees with the desire of Mrs. Ferrari—"la Signora Laura"—to have a greater say in decisions about the Scuderia. Engineer Mauro Forghieri is appointed as team principal; he will work primarily on developing the Ferrari 250 GTO.

1962

Olivier Gendebien and Phil Hill win the 24 Hours of Le Mans, held on June 23 and 24, in a Ferrari 330 TRI-LM. Two Ferrari 250 GTO, driven by the duos of Jean Guichet and Pierre Noblet, and "Eldé" and Jean Blaton (Belgian national team), cross the line second and third.

1963

Through Lee Iacocca, Ford begins final negotiations to buy Ferrari. Realizing that he will no longer have

1964 The 275 P in which Jean Guichet and Nino Vaccarella (#20) have won the 24 Hours of Le Mans.

JUNE 19–20, 1967 Arrival of the two 330 P4 (#23 and #24) and the 412 P (#26) during the 24 Hours of Daytona (Florida).

1972 Opening of the test track in Fiorano.

control over his "beloved racing cars," Enzo Ferrari ends negotiations on May 20. A few days later, Lorenzo Bandini and Ludovico Scarfiotti win the 24 Hours of Le Mans, held on June 15 and 16, in a 250 P.

At the Paris Motor Show, Ferrari unveils the 250 LM, which will become the GTO 64 a year later.

1964

Jean Guichet and Nino Vaccarella win the 24 Hours of Le Mans held on June 20 and 21 driving a 275 P. John Surtees and Lorenzo Bandini finish third in a 330 P.

Enzo Ferrari falls out with the Automobile Club d'Italia after its refusal to approve the 250 LM as a GT. As a consequence, the Scuderia's racing cars are leased by Luigi Chinetti's American NART team. They race under white and blue colors at the United States and Mexican Grands Prix, after which John Surtees becomes world champion driving a Ferrari 158, the first person to win a world championship in both grand prix motorcycle and Formula 1 racing.

The Ferrari 250 LM affair becomes a scandal in Italy and the car is finally certified as a GT. The Scuderia's Formula 1 cars are repainted red—for good—before the next Grand Prix.

1965

The 275 GTB, GT, and Competizione make their first appearances.

Victory for a Ferrari 250 LM driven by Masten Gregory and Jochen Rindt (North American Racing Team) in the 24 Hours of Le Mans, held on June 19 and 20.

1967

Lorenzo Bandini and Chris Amon (#23) win the 24 Hours of Daytona in a 330 P4, held on 19 and 20 June in Florida. They come in ahead of Ludovico Scarfiotti and Mike Parkes (#24) in another 330 P4, and Pedro Rodríguez and Jean Guichet (#26) in a 412 P.

1968

Ferrari produces its first Dino, the 206 GT, which later becomes the 246 GT, and the 375 GTB/4 Berlinetta, GT and Competizione version, nicknamed Daytona.

1969

Production begins on the Spider Daytona 365 GTS/4.

1970

On March 7, during the South African Grand Prix in Sandton, Ferrari launches the 312 B, with the first flat-12-cylinder, 3-liter engine in Formula 1, driven by Jacky Ickx.

1971

Peter Schetty becomes team principal at Scuderia Ferrari.

At Maranello, Ferrari begins work on its official, private test track, which is finished on April 8, 1972.

1972

Ferrari wins the World Endurance Championship (today's WEC) with a 312 P. At the end of the year, Peter Schetty decides that the Scuderia no longer has the

1975 Luca di Montezemolo and Niki Lauda.

1980 Jody Scheckter and Gilles Villeneuve during the official presentation of the 312 T5, Fiorano.

1987 Presentation of the F40 on the Dino Ferrari Circuit in Imola, Italy.

financial means to compete in both the Formula 1 and World Endurance Championship. Enzo Ferrari chooses to concentrate on Formula 1 from 1974.

1973

In June, Enzo Ferrari and Mauro Forghieri discuss the arrival of a new team principal to lead the Scuderia: Luca di Montezemolo.

In both the World Endurance Championship and at Le Mans, Ferrari is beaten by Matra.

1974

On April 28, Niki Lauda drives a 312 B3 to his first Grand Prix victory, at the Spanish Grand Prix in Madrid.

1975

First appearance in a Grand Prix of the Ferrari 312 T, with its new transverse gearbox.

On September 7, Niki Lauda becomes world champion at the Italian Grand Prix in Monza, eleven years after John Surtees' title. Between 1975 and 1977, Ferrari wins three successive Formula 1 constructors' championships.

1976

During the German Grand Prix in Nürburg on August 1, Niki Lauda has a near-fatal accident during which his Ferrari catches fire. He returns to competition six weeks later.

Luca di Montezemolo leaves the Scuderia for a different role within the Fiat group.

In October, Ferrari launches the BB 512 Berlinetta and 400 GT 2+2 Automatic.

1978

Marco Piccinini, an advisor to Enzo Ferrari, takes over as principal of the Scuderia.

The 308 GTB makes its rally debut, race-prepared by the Michelotto workshop, in the Targa Florio in Sicily. "Lele" Pinto gets his first victory the following spring during the Monza Rally Show. Jean-Claude Andruet, at the wheel of a 308 entered by Pozzi-France, wins the Tour de France Automobile in 1981 and 1982.

1979

The Scuderia wins the Formula 1 drivers' and constructors' championships with the T4. Jody Scheckter is champion, ahead of Gilles Villeneuve.

1980

At the Fiorano track, Mauro Forghieri asks Gilles Villeneuve to test a semi-automatic gearbox with paddle-shift controls. When asked by Enzo Ferrari if the system works, the Canadian driver replies "yes," but expresses a preference for a conventional gearshift. The project is abandoned.

The project is later rediscovered in the technical office by engineer John Barnard, Mauro Forghieri's successor. He fits it to the Ferrari 640, which wins the 1989 Brazilian Grand Prix in Rio de Janeiro. All Formula 1 cars and racing prototypes now benefit from this system.

1987 *Tribute to Ferrari* exhibition, Fondation Cartier pour l'art contemporain, Jouy-en-Josas.

1990 Alain Prost during the Australian Grand Prix in Adelaide.

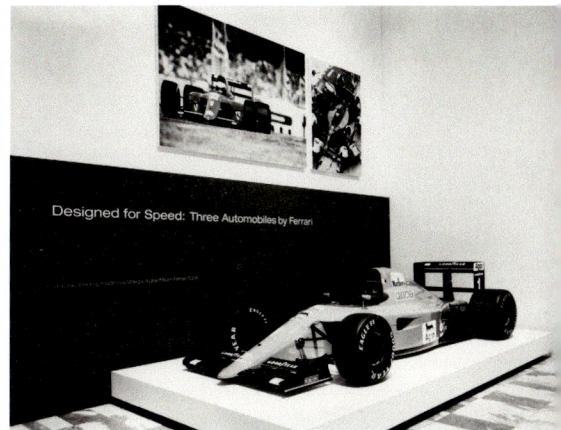

1993 *Designed for Speed: Three Automobiles by Ferrari* exhibition, MoMA, New York.

1981

The Scuderia fields two 126 CKs with turbocharged V6 engines for the first Grand Prix of the season on March 15 in Long Beach, California, joining Renault, which is also using turbocharged engines.

1982

During the darkest season in the Scuderia's history, Gilles Villeneuve is killed on May 8 during practice for the Belgian Grand Prix in Zolder, and Didier Pironi suffers a serious accident on August 7 during practice for the German Grand Prix in Hockenheim, marking the end of his Formula 1 career. Patrick Tambay replaces the Canadian and wins the Grand Prix. Despite these tragedies, Ferrari wins the constructors' world championship.

1983

Ferrari once again wins the Formula 1 constructors' championship thanks to Patrick Tambay's victory at San Marino and René Arnoux's in Canada, Germany, and the Netherlands.

1984

In March, Ferrari begins production of the 288 GTO, the predecessor of the F40.

1986

Mauro Forghieri leaves Ferrari definitively.

1987

John Barnard takes over as team principal of the Scuderia.

On May 22, the Fondation Cartier opens *Tribute to Ferrari*, an exhibition at the Domaine du Montcel in Jouy-en-Josas, in the presence of numerous public figures, including Piero Ferrari, Jean Todt, and Alain Prost.

On July 21, Ferrari officially launches the F40.

Gerhard Berger finishes the Formula 1 season with two victories, in Japan and Australia, Ferrari's first wins in a Grand Prix since August 4, 1985, when Michele Alboreto won at the Nürburgring, Germany.

1988

Enzo Ferrari dies on August 14, at the age of ninety.

1989

Cesare Fiorio, ex-sporting director of rallying at Lancia, becomes the Scuderia's new team principal.

In October, the F40 LM makes its debut at the Laguna Seca Raceway in California for Jean Sage and Daniel Marin's Ferrari France team. The car, driven by Jean Alesi, finishes third behind two four-wheel-drive Audi 90s.

1990

Alain Prost, already a three-time world champion, becomes the Scuderia's number-one driver. At the season-ending Japanese Grand Prix in Suzuka, the French driver's Ferrari 641 is deliberately shunted by Ayrton Senna's McLaren at the first corner, handing the Brazilian the world title.

OCTOBER 8, 2000 Michael Schumacher and Jean Todt during the Japanese Grand Prix in Suzuka.

2002 The Ferrari Enzo, Fiorano Circuit.

2013 The LaFerrari, Fiorano Circuit.

On June 8, Ferrari inaugurates *L'idea Ferrari* at Florence's Forte di Belvedere, the first major exhibition dedicated to the car manufacturer in Italy.

1991

Luca di Montezemolo returns to Ferrari as chair and asks the company's engineers to concentrate on making Ferraris more suitable for everyday use. As a result, the Testa Rossa is modified to become the 512 TR.

1993

On Niki Lauda's advice, Luca di Montezemolo asks Jean Todt to take over the Scuderia. "The Scuderia Ferrari is a castle," Todt says, "but a castle in ruins." The former director of Peugeot Talbot Sport sets about turning the team around.

On November 4, the exhibition, *Designed for Speed: Three Automobiles by Ferrari*, opens at MoMA in New York, featuring a 166 MM Barchetta, an F40, and a Ferrari 641 that competed in the 1990 F1, as well as over sixty design drawings. The 641 is then placed on permanent display, following a donation by Ferrari.

1995

Ferrari begins production of the Ferrari F50 with its naturally aspirated, 4.7-liter V12 engine to mark the Prancing Horse's fiftieth anniversary.

1996

Jean Todt signs Michael Schumacher and Eddie Irvine to replace Gerhard Berger and Jean Alesi, and introduces the 90° V10 Formula 1 engine.

On June 2, at the Spanish Grand Prix in Barcelona, Michael Schumacher wins his first race for Ferrari.

1997

Ferrari acquires Maserati, the Prancing Horse's historical rival in Formula 1 and sports cars in the 1950s.

The Ferrari 355 F1 is the first road-going Ferrari equipped with a semi-automatic gearbox, similar to Formula 1 cars.

On October 26 at the European Grand Prix in Jerez, Jacques Villeneuve in a Williams-Renault is crowned world champion following a collision with Michael Schumacher in a Ferrari. Deemed at fault for the crash, the Ferrari driver is later disqualified from the championship.

1999

Ferrari is again crowned Formula 1 constructors' champion, Jean Todt's first title.

2000

Michael Schumacher and Ferrari win the first of five consecutive Formula 1 drivers' and constructors' world championship titles (2000, 2001, 2002, 2003, and 2004).

2002

Ferrari begins production and sales of the Ferrari Enzo with its 6-liter V12 engine; only 399 Enzos are produced.

2024 Second consecutive victory of the Hypercar 499 P in the 24 Hours of Le Mans.

2025 Lewis Hamilton wins the Sprint race at the Chinese Grand Prix in Shanghai.

2006

Launch of the 90° V8 Formula 1 engine.

2007

Kimi Räikkönen signs for Ferrari and finishes the season as the Formula 1 world champion. With this victory, Jean Todt leaves the Scuderia and is replaced by Stefano Domenicali.

2010

Ferrari revives the GTO badge with the 599 GTO, which features a 6-liter V12 producing 670 hp.

2013

With its 6.3-liter V12 and electric motor producing 963 hp, the LaFerrari becomes the first hybrid in the company's history. Only 499 are produced.

2014

Ferrari develops the 059 4-cylinder, 90° V-angle petrol engine, accompanied by an electric motor, the first hybrid in Formula 1.

At the end of the season, Luca de Montezemolo leaves Ferrari and is replaced as chair by Sergio Marchionne.

2015

Ferrari debuts on the New York Stock Exchange in October.

2016

Ferrari begins production of the F12 Tour de France with its 6.2-liter V12 producing 780 hp; 799 are produced. It has an active rear axle and a lighter body thanks to the use of carbon fiber.

2023

On January 9, Frédéric Vasseur takes over from Mattia Binotto as team principal of the Scuderia, becoming the second Frenchman to lead the Formula 1 team.

The SF90 Stradale, with its twin-turbo V8 engine combined with three electric motors, became the most powerful Ferrari in history: 1,030 hp in the XX version.

2024

Ferrari signs seven-time world champion and Mercedes driver Lewis Hamilton for the 2025 season.

On June 15 and 16, Antonio Fuoco, Nicklas Nielsen, and Miguel Molina of the AF Corse official team win the 24 Hours of Le Mans for Ferrari in a 499 P.

In October, Ferrari announces the production of 799 F80s continuing the line of supercars begun forty years earlier with the 288 GTO and the legendary F40.

2025

Lewis Hamilton wins the sprint race with the Ferrari SF-25 at the Chinese Grand Prix in Shanghai in March. It is his first victory for the Scuderia.

On June 15, Ferrari wins the 24 Hours of Le Mans for the twelfth time, the third consecutive time with the 499 P, driven by Robert Kubica, Yifei Ye and Philip Hanson (AF Corse Team).

AFTERWORD

John Elkann
President of Ferrari

In 1987 I was eleven years old and, behind my young eyes, I was already dreaming of Ferraris.

I admired the beautiful models in my grandfather Gianni Agnelli's garage. He had a great passion for the Prancing Horse and, as a personal friend of Enzo Ferrari, he would order bespoke and unique cars. I followed the Formula 1 World Championship: these were the days of Michele Alboreto and Gerhard Berger—not hugely fortunate in terms of results, but no less exciting in the eyes of a young fan. And above all—but I would only realize this later—1987 was the year in which one of the most iconic models in Ferrari's history came to life. The F40 was the last car to bear the signature of our founder: a model that would change the paradigm of supercars and is still one of our best-loved today.

This is why reliving the great exhibition *Tribute to Ferrari* that the Fondation Cartier pour l'art contemporain created has a special resonance for me.

The event, so vividly remembered in this beautiful book, was an unforgettable experience for those who were present, and a proud moment for the Italian firm. It was the first time that a world-renowned luxury house had dedicated such an important space to Ferrari.

Cartier and Ferrari, despite their distinct identities and different products, have much in common. They were born exactly a century apart: Cartier in 1847 and Ferrari in 1947. Both founders, Louis-François Cartier and Enzo Ferrari, were driven by a great passion and an iron will in the pursuit of perfection. And even after their passing, the houses they founded have continued to thrive. Their concern for tradition makes them a driving force for innovation. Whether an exquisite piece of jewelry or a unique sports car, their goal remains to achieve excellence in everything they do. MODENA, 2025

This book is dedicated to the *Tribute to Ferrari* exhibition, presented from May 22 to August 30, 1987 at the Fondation Cartier pour l'art contemporain, in Jouy-en-Josas.

This exhibition enjoyed the unconditional support of Enzo Ferrari, who enthusiastically accepted to be the patron of the event at the Fondation Cartier.

EXHIBITION

ARTISTIC DIRECTION
Marie-Claude Beaud

SCENOGRAPHY
Andrée Putman
Agence Ecart: Bruno Moinard, Dominique Voisin, Dominique Verger

THE EXHIBITION WAS CREATED IN CLOSE COLLABORATION WITH
Association Mas du Clos, Pietro de Franchi, Franco Gozzi, Piero Ferrari, Daniel Marin, Luca Matteoni, Marco Piccinini, Lorenza Pininfarina, Sergio Pininfarina, Lorenzo Ramaciotti, Giovan Battista, Razelli, Carlo Renzi, Jack Setton, Fredi Valentini and Agence VU' (Christian Caujolle and Marcel Lefranc)

PHOTOGRAPHERS
Alain Bizos, Agnès Bonnot, Pierre-Olivier Deschamps, Franco Fontana, Pascal Dolémieux, Frank Horvat, Xavier Lambours, François Le Diascorn, Erica Lennard, Jeanloup Sieff

CONTRIBUTORS
Valério Adami, Jim Palette, Bruno Pons, Fabrizio Pasquero, Antoine Prunet, Michel Tourlière, Claude Vialard, Marc Walter

BOOK

EDITOR
Philippe Séclier

EDITORIAL DIRECTOR
Pierre-Édouard Couton

FONDATION CARTIER POUR L'ART CONTEMPORAIN
Adeline Pelletier, Heritage Director
Cécile Provost, Publishing Department Manager
Flore Langlade, Publishing Coordinator
Roxane Paillou, Publishing Assistant

ATELIER EXB
Jordan Alves, Editor
Charlotte Debiolles, Production Manager

GRAPHIC DESIGN
Nolwen Lauzanne

TRANSLATION FROM ITALIAN
E.P.A. Language Services Ltd.

TRANSLATION FROM FRENCH
Tom Ridgway
Anna Knight

ENGLISH COPY EDITING
Marc Feustel, Anna Knight

COLOR SEPARATION
Clément Regard, Les Artisans du Regard, Paris

ACKNOWLEDGMENTS

The Fondation Cartier pour l'art contemporain and Philippe Séclier express their deep gratitude to Ferrari, and especially to John Elkann and Piero Ferrari. We also thank warmly Daniele Bresciani, Michele Pignatti, Francesco Giacintucci, Paolo Lorenzi, Elisa Calzolari, and Gabriele Lalli.

We wish to thank Jean-Louis Moncet, Francesca Picchi, and Jean Todt for their invaluable contributions.

We are indebted to those who accepted to share their memories of the exhibition with us and their knowledge of the models that were displayed: Marie-Claude Beaud, Christine Borgoltz, Christian Caujolle, Hervé Chandès, Pierre-Olivier Deschamps, François Le Diascorn, Daniel Marin, Bruno Moinard, Hervé Poulain, Jack Setton, Claude Vialard, and Emmanuel Zurini.

Our thanks also go to Manon Affairoux, Museo Baracca, Paul-Henri Cahier, Fabrice Connen (agence DPPI), Nicolas Delage, Pascal Dolémieux, Toni Faiola, Franco Fontana, Stéphane Foulon, Fiammetta Horvat, Virginie Laguens, Aurélie Laure, Monique Le Saint, Vanja Merhar, Alain Prost, Olivia Putman, Johnny Rives, David Saussol, and Jean-Marc Teissèdre.

CREDITS

This book was published with the kind permission of Ferrari.

This book was published by
Fondation Cartier pour l'art contemporain
2, place du Palais-Royal
75001 Paris
fondationcartier.com

ISBN: 978-2-86925-192-2

Distributed in the USA and Canada by
ARTBOOK | D.A.P.
75 Broad Street, Suite 630
New York, NY 10004
USA
www.artbook.com

Distributed in all other countries by
Thames & Hudson Ltd
6 – 24 Britannia Street
London WC1X 9JD
United Kingdom
www.thamesandhudson.com

Printed and bound in June 2025 by
Offsetdruckerei Karl Grammlich,
Pliezhausen, Germany

Legal deposit: October 2025